Praying Hyde
A Man of Prayer

Praying Hyde

The story of John Hyde
missionary to India

Basil Miller

Ambassador International
GREENVILLE, SOUTH CAROLINA & BELFAST, NORTHERN IRELAND

Praying Hyde
A Man of Prayer

© 2008 Ambassador International
All rights reserved
Printed in the United States of America

Cover design by David Siglin of A&E Media

ISBN 978-1-932307-89-4

Published by the Ambassador Group

Ambassador International
427 Wade Hampton Blvd.
Greenville, SC 29609
USA
www.emeraldhouse.com

and

Ambassador Publications Ltd.
Providence House
Ardenlee Street
Belfast BT6 8QJ
Northern Ireland
www.ambassador-productions.com

The colophon is a trademark of Ambassador

CONTENTS

CHAPTER   PAGE

  I Deep-Laid Roots 7

 II Beginning The India Trek.............. 15

III Molding The Man..................... 33

 IV United For Prayer.................... 47

  V Forward Through Prayer.............. 62

 VI Following The Gleam.................. 80

VII The Harvest of His Prayers........... 96

VIII Along The Indian Road...............109

 IX Edging Toward The Heavenly Kingdom..120

  X Shouting The Victory 128

Chapter I

DEEP-LAID ROOTS

They called him "the man who never sleeps." Some termed him "the apostle of prayer," but more familiarly he is known as "Praying Hyde." John Hyde was all of these and more, for deep in India's Punjab he envisioned his Master, and face to face with the Eternal he learned lessons of prayer which to others were amazing. Walking on such anointed ground for days without leaving the throne of prayer, John held holy converse with his Lord.

When he returned to field preaching from such seasons of tranquil repose, his sword was keen for he had sharpened it with prayer. He was thus possessed of a spiritual power which opened dark hearts of India to his message.

Seeing him pray for thirty days and nights, or ten days on end, or remain on his knees for thirty-six hours without moving, fellow workers beheld him first in awe, then disgust, finally to be filled with admiration for this apostle of intercession and to sit at his feet as disciples.

Hyde opened heaven's windows upon his own soul through faith and prayer, and while they were thrown back others looked through and glimpsed eternal glories. Said missionaries who thus sat with Hyde when those gates were ajar, "We could never be the same again." Mary Campbell, who for forty-five years walked India's dusty roads, traversing every province, told me, "John Hyde taught us that prayer avails . . . that prayer still is the Christian's most powerful instrument in India, in America, in all the world.''

That was Praying Hyde, the man of whom an Indian missionary affirmed, "It is a good thing John Hyde was not buried in India, for the non-Christians would have made a shrine of his grave." After thirty years of rest from his labors the mark of the man is still deep in India's heart. For he not only won individuals for Christ, but with his spirit and emblem of prayer he sweetened the entire stream of missionary endeavor.

Though dead these three decades, Praying Hyde's soul lives on in the land of his love and labors. Although his earthly ministry has ceased, the power of his achievement in India and America is greater today than ever during his career.

John was a son of the manse, where his life was early cultured in an atmosphere of prayer. For many years his father, Smith Hyde, was a spiritually-minded Presbyterian minister in Illinois. As a man of rare balance and proportion, his soul was healthful, genial and virile, and his ministry was stamped with godliness. His attainments were humble though scholarly, and for seventeen years he marshaled the Presbyterian forces in Carthage, Illinois, the seat of Carthage College. Smith was a loving husband, a courteous leader and a true father to his half dozen children, three boys and an equal number of girls.

Mothering the group was a sweet-spirited, music-loving, high-minded lady of gentle birth, whose influence was indirect like the pervading rays of sun which burst with joy and beauty the tenderest flowers.

Into this family John was born on November 9, 1865, at Carrollton in the state where the foundation of his father's ministerial service was to be laid. John lived the life characteristic of an Illinois preacher's son until the family moved to Carthage in 1882.

He learned to love the ring of his godly father's voice in the public pulpit as he declared the saving Gospel of power. He listened as that noble man of God lifted the vision of the ripened soul-fields into which the Lord of harvest was to send forth laborers. It was not in public concourse, however, that Father Hyde was to make the greatest impression upon his son.

Around the family altar Smith helped to shape the soul of young John, when the father raised his voice heavenward and called upon God to greet with divine dews his petition. And how that father could pray! "He was a noble man of God," says Francis McGaw, a friend of the family who later dipped his pen in his own heart of love and told the simple story of Praying Hyde. "I have frequently heard Dr. Hyde pray the Lord to thrust out laborers into His harvest. He would pray this prayer both at the family altar and from his pulpit."

It was around that family altar that God planted the roots from which Praying Hyde's marvelous life of intercession was to flourish. Had there been no life-molding family altar where young John's soul met the Master day by day under the thrill of his father's Spirit-charged voice, there would have

been no Praying Hyde as we know him. God goes
back in the producing of Johns and Timothies to
Father Smith as well as Grandmother Lois and
Mother Eunice.

"Often I have knelt with them and have . . . been
strangely moved when dear Mr. Hyde poured out
his heart to God as he prayed at the family altar,"
says McGaw, then a young minister. No less was
son John strangely moved by his father's words
as they winged their way toward the glory world.

The year the family moved to Carthage, John,
high in hope, entered the local college, from which
he graduated with such high honors that he was
elected to a teaching position on the college faculty.
Professor John, however, had heard the Voice, and
shortly laying aside the scholastic robes he had
donned, he matriculated at the Presbyterian Seminary in Chicago, then known as McCormick.

John was wise enough to be a professor, but in
God's plan for his life he needed the seasoning of
the seminary, where his vision was to sweep from
America to India as the scene of his labors. He had
been preceded at McCormick by an older brother
Edmund, with whom he was to spend two years of
unbroken fellowship.

During his student days he planned to be a minister and in an unobtrusive manner he was consci-
entiously carrying out the design. His fellow
students, affirms Burton Konkle, then also a semi-
narian, thought of him as one who would settle in
a small and ordinary pastorate and do a grand but
inconspicuous piece of work. It was not until his
senior year that he was looked upon as traveling

toward a different destiny. "And doubtless he would have been one of the last men in the class of whom more would have been expected," affirms Konkle.

The class had been active in city and foreign missions from the very first. Hyde however took only a mild interest in these programs, for his soul until then had not been touched by the flame of overseas kingdom work. One evening early in the semester, the usual missionary meeting was held by the students in the chapel. The voice of Herrick Johnson had been most appealing.

Hyde left that service with a stirring within his heart. God had been speaking and John could not remain still. He went to see Konkle, who had participated in the program that night. Sitting down in Konkle's room, he remained silent for some time and then said, "Give me all the arguments you have for the foreign field."

Konkle returned, "You know as much about foreign missions as I do. Arguments are not what you need. What you want to do is go to your room, get down on your knees, and stay there until the matter is settled one way or another."

Hyde left the room and returned to his own — not to sleep but to fight the battle through to a finish. So well did he battle with God and the lost world as his parish that the next morning, as he met his friends just as they were going into the chapel, there was a ring of decisiveness in his voice as he said, "It's settled, Konkle."

Previously his own brother had answered the call to become a student volunteer, but he was not per-

mitted to live. The blow set John wondering what
he might do to take his brother Edmund's place.
Once that battle was fought John was not long in
getting into the missionary harness. As he said
those words of surrender, "I'll go where you want
me to go, dear Lord," John Hyde meant it from the
farthest reaches of his inner being.

He began to talk missions, pray missions, herald
missions, buttonhole fellow classmates for missions.
He here began his wonderful ministry of personal
persuasion which was to be so successful in India
soul-winning. One by one he took classmates for
long walks, when he poured into their hearts the
vision which God had painted on the canvas of his
own memory.

And those walks became fruitful of decisions until
when graduation time came in the spring of 1892,
twenty-six out of the forty-six seniors had pledged
themselves for foreign service. In all these John
was the prime influence which shunted men from
home to foreign lands.

Here John laid the foundation for his wonderful
life of prayer. Behind every man who made his
decision for missionary work was John's prayer
that he might take this step. He bathed his spirit in
intercession, and so well did John accomplish that
work, that one wonders if the greatest results of his
personal ministry did not spring from the labors
of the men whose lives he slanted by prayer toward
the foreign field.

One student, Lee, went to Korea, having been in-
fluenced by John's prayers, and in more than thirty
years' work built sixty-seven churches.

Such a man as John could not long remain in-
active, and as soon as he had tucked his seminary
diploma into a moldy old trunk or musty attic, he
made plans for his glorious pilgrimage to India's
shores. He knew where God would have him work,
and with this vision his support was not long in
coming.

Martha Gray, John's classmate at Carthage, was
secretary of the Carthage presbytery young people's
work, and when it was known that John was India-
bound, the group underwrote his support. From
that time on until after his death, Miss Gray assumed this obligation, faithfully discharging it even
to the raising of a five-thousand-dollar John Hyde
Memorial Fund, of which we shall speak later.

Between them they formed the plan that three
or four times a year John was to write Martha, and
she in turn was to copy the letters for local society
distribution. Thus while John was in India, Martha
held his American ropes, as Andrew Fuller did for
his friend William Carey. Those letters were to
come with spasmodic regularity until John returned
home to die in 1912.

It is indeed a mistake to think of John's prayer
life as beginning in India during 1904 when the
Punjab Prayer Union was formed, for John since
his seminary days was always an apostle of intercession. His senior-year seminary intercession alone
wrought for the kingdom in such momentous manner
that foreign missions received therefrom twenty-six
workmen.

Nor was John long to remain in the homeland, for
he had heard the call, and was not content until he

too should go. Praying himself into the divine will, he found no difficulty in praying his way to India, which is indeed what he accomplished.

Graduating in the spring, he was ready to sail for Bombay by October 15. He bid his praying father adieu, upon whose gentle face he was never to look again, and set sail for India that he might take the place of his brother, as William Knibbs was to take the place of his brother in Jamaica, and Father Damien, the leper priest, was to give his life instead of a brother who also had died in a faraway land.

Had he dampened the ardor of his soul to such an extent he could have remained content in America, he might have fulfilled his classmate's idea of him — "settle in a small church and carry on a conventional work."

Heeding the heavenly vision, he was to hold aloft in India the torch of prayer so that others could thereby have their pathway lighted into the kingdom of which God is the Ruler.

CHAPTER II

BEGINNING THE INDIA TREK

It was a grand group of missionaries that John met at New York City on October 15, 1892. Leaving home and friends behind — friends whom he was not to see for ten years — he was not to sail alone. On the ship were five other missionaries, John Forman and wife, and Mr. and Mrs. C. R. Janvier, as well as an unmarried missionary, Sarah Wherry. Fifteen days later the ship docked at Liverpool, to tie up at Bombay during the end of November.

"There was little that occurred during the voyage to give one any thought of what John Hyde was to become as a spiritual influence," says Sarah Wherry, looking back fifty years to the journey. "To be sure, he was very serious, carefully conscientious in all religious matters, but he did not in any way suggest leadership. He kept himself modest and was retiring, though not a recluse."

This was the outward John. Inwardly there was a raging tempest sweeping the ocean of his soul. He had thought of himself as a missionary fledgling, on his way to a marvelous adventure. He had given attention to many things, such as a wide seminary training, and a missionary zeal in winning recruits to his favorite profession. But he had not been sufficiently diligent in the development of what was to count most as a qualifying factor for his twenty-year career.

Diligent in mind-building, he had forgotten to polish his own soul with the care God demanded. This was to be brought forcibly home to him on the India voyage. Later he told the story to a missionary co-laborer, J. Pengwern Jones.

"My father was a minister and my mother a very devoted Christian," he says, "with a beautiful voice which had been consecrated to the Lord. I determined when a youth to be a missionary, and a 'good missionary.' I wanted to shine as a great missionary . . .

"I determined to master the Indian languages that I would have to learn, and I resolved not to let anything stand in the way that would hinder my becoming a great missionary.

"That was my ambition"— an ambition out of which he had left the main factor: God. "This was perhaps not altogether of the flesh, but most of it was. I loved the Lord and wanted to serve Him and serve Him well, but 'self' was at the foundation of my ambition."

John's father had a minister friend, who in his early days was possessed of a consuming desire to be a missionary, but circumstances shunted his services to a homeland pastorate. This friend on learning of John's India venture was greatly interested in him. "He loved me and I loved . . . and admired him," says John.

"When I got on board the steamer at New York," says the young missionary, resuming the story, "bound for India for my life work, I found in my cabin a letter addressed to me. It was in the handwriting of my father's friend. I opened and read it."

It was not a long letter but the words leaped at John, burrowed into the depths of his soul, set there a flame of indignation upon the ashes of his pride. Said the minister friend, "I shall not cease praying for you, dear John, until you are filled with the Holy Spirit." The Holy Spirit — that expression was to face John many times until at length he became fully filled and dynamically conscious of the Spirit.

"My pride was touched," John says of the incident, "and I felt exceedingly angry, crushed the letter, threw it into a corner of the cabin and went up on deck in a very angry spirit. The idea of implying that I was *not* filled with the Spirit!"

John was going as a missionary, he told himself, and it was presumptuous for him to go without being filled with the Holy Spirit; he was headed for the top, was he not? and as a natural condition, he thought himself Spirit-filled.

"And yet this man implied that I was not fitted and equipped for the work! I paced up and down that deck, a battle raging within. I felt very uncomfortable; I loved the writer, I knew the holy life he lived, and down in my heart was the conviction that he was right and that I was not fitted to be a missionary."

This was a battle not soon to be won, nor was John so constituted that he could turn from the fray with anything less than victory. He went back to his cabin, on his knees searched for the thrust-aside missive, and, finding it, smoothed the paper out "and read it again and again. I still felt annoyed, but the conviction was gaining on me that my father's friend was right and I was wrong."

In this condition he was near to believing ground.
The searching went on for a few days, during which
John's soul was a tumult of misery. He refers to
this turbulency of spirit as the goodness of God in
answering his friend's prayer.

"At last in despair, I asked the Lord to fill me
with the Holy Spirit, and the moment I did this,
the whole atmosphere was cleared up. I began to
see myself and what a selfish ambition I had. It was
a struggle almost to the end of the voyage, but I
was determined long before the port was reached,
that whatever the cost, I would be really filled with
the Spirit. The second climax came when I was led
to tell the Lord I was willing even to fail in my
language examinations in India, and be a missionary
working quietly out of sight, that I would do anything and be anything, but the Holy Spirit I would
have at any cost."

When John arrived in India this soul-quest was
not at an end. He was invited to attend an open-air
service where a missionary was the speaker. The
sermon went directly to John's conscience, and at
once the heavenly voice told him the message was
about Jesus Christ as a real Saviour from sin. At
the close of the service an Englishman walked to
the speaker and asked whether he himself had been
thus saved.

That was the soul-moving question which John
dared not face. "The question went home to my
heart; for if it had been asked me, I would have had
to confess that Christ had not fully saved *me*, because I knew that there was a sin in my life which
had not been taken away. I realized what a dishonor

it would be on the Name of Christ to have to confess that I was preaching a Christ that had not delivered me from sin, though I was proclaiming to others that He was a perfect Saviour.''

John's soul was mired in the Slough of Despond. Himself proclaiming a full salvation, he had not experienced the joy of this great redemption. Going back to his room, he shut himself in and told God that he must do one of two things. ''Either Thou must give me the victory over all my sins, and especially over the sin that so easily besets me, or I shall return to America and seek there for some other work. I am unable to preach the Gospel until I can testify of its power in my own life.''

John had met the condition laid down for the forgiveness of sins, that of confession, and he cast his soul upon the message from John's epistle, ''If we confess . . . He is faithful and just to forgive.'' For some time he faced the issue, knowing well that his soul was on the path which led to Calvary and victory over sin.

Then God whispered, with the voice of assurance that He was willing and able to deliver him from all sin, and that he was to perform a divinely planned work in India. The Almighty had spoken, and victory flushed the life of John, who says, ''He did deliver me, and I have not had a doubt of this since. I can now stand up without hesitation to testify that He has given me victory, and I love to witness to this and to tell all of the wonderful faithfulness of Christ my Lord, my Saviour.''

While thus relating the experience to his friend Pengwern Jones, John's face shone with the light of glory bursting upon it. "Can I ever forget his face as he told me these things, that inexpressibly sad look when he spoke of his sin, and that wonderful smile of his when he referred to the faithfulness of Christ?" asked Jones, whose early memories of Praying Hyde were first published in India.

With this soul-victory over sin, John was ready for work. Twelve years were to pass before he began to gather in the glorious harvest of his prayers. During this time he was to labor unnoticed and unsung, an ordinary man in an ordinary manner, praying the while, trusting and laying the foundation through service which would fit him for a position of respect and prayer renown in India.

He was not to climb those golden stairs of prayer fame at once, but was to toughen the fiber of his soul through nights of haunting danger, hours of praying face downward when the answer seemed far away, trust amid difficulties through which the eye of faith could not pierce.

But John went about those duties, faithful in the small responsibilities, willing to be an unknown worker in God's enterprises. At first John did nothing remarkable, nothing out of the ordinary, and showed little genius for organization. He was slightly hard of hearing and this no doubt handicapped him in mastering the language rapidly. Gentle of disposition, he had little trouble adjusting himself to the other workers in the Ferozepore district.

His first task was language study, of which work only occasional glimpses are given. He was located at Dehra Dun where Dr. Ullman was the teacher.

While engaged in this task, a revelation dawned
upon him. He had come to India to teach the dark-
minded natives of Christ, whose glory bursts from
the Bible. Yet he did not know the Bible.

At once he determined to master the Word of
God that he might thereby better present the
Saviour to India's hordes. This tangled him in a
slight difficulty with the examining board. Missionaries with whom I have talked who knew John
during those early years, such as Mary Campbell,
say that he was slow in learning Hindustani. This
came not from a linguistic inaptitude, but from the
fact that he neglected language for Bible study. And
when the committee reprimanded him, and even
threatened to reject him on the field, he quietly replied, "I must put first things first."

That was all there was to it, and he felt that before anything else must come a complete working
mastery of the Bible. Universally missionaries testify that John became fluent in the speech of his
adopted land. He had come to India to teach God's
Word and he asked the Holy Spirit to open it to his
spiritual discernment. Once this was done John
was ready and willing to leap the language hurdles
as they came to him.

"He became a correct and easy speaker in Urdu,
Junjabi, as well as his own native speech," writes
a friend, who heard him discourse to large audiences. "And above all that he mastered the language
of heaven, and so learned to speak that he held
audiences of hundreds of Indians spellbound while
he opened to them the truths of God's Word."

Mary Campbell, who herself had mastered enough of the many languages and dialects of India to enable her to preach to 200,000,000 Indians, says that Praying Hyde presented on the platform a noble appearance, and spoke the dialect of the people with such ease that the smoothness of his words almost marked him as a native.

John wrote his college magazine a letter in 1894 in which he gives us a glimpse of his early work. "Last year (1893) until June 1, I was at my station studying Hindustani, then I went to the Himalayas for three weeks . . . saw many missionaries and enjoyed it. The rest of the time till November 15 I spent in Dehra Dun. I was studying there with Mr. Ullman . . . a fine teacher, and his spiritual influence was most helpful to me. A distinct blessing came to me there after months of seeking.

"The blood of Jesus now had to me a power not realized before. Most of the winter and spring until today was spent among the villages with Indian preachers. Yesterday eight low caste persons were baptized at one of the villages. It seems a work in which man, even as an instrument, was used in a very small degree.

"Pray for us. I learn to speak the language very, very slowly; can talk only a little in public or in conversation. For my classmates I pray constantly. Will not some of you come out this year? The laborers are few — so few."

It was during these days, when the language was slow in reaching the degree of fluency which would permit him to work with the natives, that he offered his resignation to the Synod, saying that because of deafness he could not learn the speech of the people.

At once the Synod was faced with a petition from the village people where he had been laboring begging them not to accept the resignation, saying, "If he never speaks the language of our lips, he speaks the language of our hearts." There could be but one reply to such a request, and John's continued presence among the villagers was that answer. He remained to the end with them.

From the beginning of his work John was a village missionary, whose duty was the evangelization of villages where stationed workers could not be sent. To this task he remained true even to the end. The details of his many journeys are lacking, but day in and day out, through months into the years, even two decades, John Hyde took his little tent in which he lived, and accompanied by such native workers as were available, traveled from village to village speaking the language of heaven to the hearts of the Indians.

He had thus no permanent abode, except for a room here or there with missionary friends; so his dying request was that a fund be raised to build a missionary home where the workers could be stationed in comfort. This, as shall appear later, was accomplished.

But with that tent John was completely at home. He lived in it, slept in it, carried it with him and made it an anteroom to heaven's open portals. A letter to Martha Gray, that she in turn copied for the young people's societies which carried Hyde's support, opens the door to some of his early activities and desires.

"At my last writing I was in Dehra," he says in a letter written at Ferozepore under date of January 2, 1894. "I remained there until about the middle of November, coming down then to our Annual Mission Meeting in Ludhiana ... It was good to meet the missionaries again . . . In the Annual Meeting itself there is a great deal of business. Missionary work presents many difficulties, calling for much sympathy, it seems to me, with the older missionaries who bear the burden of the work. Our morning prayer meetings were good. Dr. Lucas led one, and he spoke about our giving ourselves continually to prayer and ministry of the Word . . .

"The way into the district work (village visitation) has been kept open for me. It is the work I would like to do. In this Ferozepore district with its six or seven hundred thousand people, the district work is outside the city with its twenty thousand. These district people live in hundreds of villages and towns . . .

"In this district are two sub-stations, at Huktsar and Moga . . . For catechists (native workers) to preach in and around these centers all the year, and for us who care to itinerate among the villages and towns from these and other good centers in the cold season is the way the Gospel is preached to hundreds of thousands.

"The field is barren of conversions, but the Lord sends His laborers into the harvest."

John goes on to outline the assistance he has in carrying on this village visitation. There are five men in all, himself and another missionary, along with three native workers. He says, "Suppose Chicago were a heathen city and yourself one of fifteen to preach the Gospel to its million and a half people. I don't know, but I believe as you prayed for strength you would also pray earnestly for laborers."

This is the burden for laborers which he passed on to the Christian young people who supported him. "Why should not one of your Society come out to the foreign field this year? Why should not you come? It is not I whom you answer, but the Lord."

During this year he lived with a missionary family, the Newtons, when he could be rightly said to live anywhere outside of the villages to which he carried his message. One happy association came about through the Newton daughter who had "been breathing the good air of Mr. Moody's Chicago Institute and the Northfield Student gatherings — places where the Spirit has been pleased to bless many."

During the year 1893 he refers to two beneficences: good health wherein he had been free from fever, and the influence of Dr. Ullman which largely touched his spiritual life. Then he adds, "For Mr. F. B. Meyer's book, *Christian Living,* and for your prayers . . . "

The preacher in Hyde emerged as he thought of his Christian Endeavor supporters in Illinois. Offering his testimony, he says, "It is good to know the Saviour better. Not so much that He is ours as that we are His. It is good just to take God at His

Word and realize that Jesus Christ . . . His own self
bear our sins, all our sins, in His own body on the
tree; that he that believeth hath everlasting life;
that there is therefore now no condemnation; that
now we are the sons of God. It is good to have as
the best of memory's trysting places a certain old
place called Calvary . . . ''

John, carrying a prayer burden for India, also
urged his Endeavor friends to pray and learn the
joyous art of trusting God for home blessings and
showers of grace on India. Closing his letter he
appended notes from other writers, such as, ''A man
who said that he felt sorry for the heathen was asked
by an old Quaker, 'Friend, didst thou feel in the
right place? Didst thou feel in thy pocket?' '' He
also refers to Bishop Whipple's statement, ''There
is no failure in Christian work; the only failure is
in not doing it.''

Again he passed along General Armstrong's
words, ''What are Christians put into the world
for except to do the impossible in the strength of
God?''

This reveals the heart of Praying Hyde. He
was laboring daily in the strength of God, trying to
achieve the impossible through Him. Later in a
letter to Martha Gray he refers to the trying heat
of India's summers, and says that only by drinking
daily at the fount of divine strength could he
carry on.

The following year was one of personal victory
which he pictures in a letter to the McCormick magazine. During this time we find him associated with
Dr. Martin of Lahore, working both in that district

and his original one. He speaks of his labors being among "the countless villages and towns, containing probably 1,200,000 people, but especially among the low castes, whose numbers I think will reach 200,000. They are from the despised serf element of almost all villages, and are degraded enough to eat the flesh of animals that die of themselves."

In the Lahore district there was a native Christian element of possibly four hundred members in ten villages. In this district a few of these had been baptized during the current year of 1895. His task was to minister to the Christians along with the others who made up the villages.

"I know the work here in Lauke best, so will try to picture it to you," he says, delineating the joyous task of winning Indians to his Master. "The low caste Christian teacher here and a man of a near village discussed together for some time last summer, with no results. Our teacher gave him a New Testament, for better than most, he could read. He told me the other day that when he came to the words, 'Heaven and earth shall pass away: but my words shall not pass away,' then he was convinced. Now he is himself one of our teachers."

Hyde, ever since arriving in India and planting his feet on the solid Rock of redemption, had been praying for a revival among the people. It was during this year that he was to have a glimpse of the work, which however was not to come to full fruition until the Sialkot revival beginning about 1905.

"God gave us a little revival season here for some two or three weeks in January. In these same meet-

ings I remember one low caste man's face and mind
seemed to take in the Word — literally to drink it
in, and I was given such simpleness and clearness of
expression that I wonder at it yet.''

Most blessed of all were the early morning prayer
meetings during those weeks when the men learned
to pray, of which Hyde says, "This will let you see
a little of the work that is most encouraging. We
would like to see similar things in each of the villages where there are Christians.''

Nor was all smooth sailing, for the non-Christians
tried to keep the water-carriers from bringing John
water each day. In his little tent he took the matter
to the Lord, and the natives "stole from us, and
threatened to pull down our tents, all apparently to
get us away. They have succeeded in taking the
house our teacher occupied, so we have no place
for a teacher here. Last Saturday night one of the
Christians was beaten, and they threaten them all
with such sufferings that these are times of trouble
and trial of faith.

"I have been much at the Throne — I have needed
to go for myself, too — but it is a Throne of Grace.''

Those were growing days for John's spiritual
man. He was learning to trust not in himself but
in the Lord. "Since coming to India, God has given
me an understanding with Himself. He apparently
is ready to bless the missionaries, workers, Christians and non-Christians, and especially the low
castes. Pray in faith for immediate blessings in
India. Wilder has been among us some of the past
year''— doubtless he was the sire of the Student
Volunteer Movement and a Princetonian.

"He was in Lahore in February, and we hear that Dr. Ewing, president of our college there, has received the Pentecostal gift, and that others have entered in. Praise the Lord."

During the following year John R. Mott conducted college conferences in the Punjab, and at one of these John Hyde delivered an address to the students. The message gives an insight into Hyde's thinking and lifts the curtain that obscures his soul.

"It also happens at times," he said, "that we do not see the fruit of our labors, and the heart longs to see the harvest." This doubtless comes from John's own experience, for later he refers to the fact that while there were conversions during 1895, there were none in 1896.

Continuing, he relates, "I have read a story of a Scottish preacher to whom one Sabbath morning some of the elders came and said they felt they ought to speak to him about the small results of the past year. The minister told them that only one twelve-year-old boy was received as a communicant. But the boy came to the minister and asked, 'Pastor, do you think if I worked hard I could be a minister, and a missionary perhaps?' 'Robert,' said the minister, 'you have healed the wound in my heart. Yes, I think you will be a missionary.'

"Years passed and a great crowd gathered to hear a returned missionary. Large audiences greeted him and the noble stood uncovered in his presence. It was Robert Moffat, the boy of the old Kirk. He had added a country to civilization, a province to the Church and savages through his work had become obedient to Christ.

"The harvest of faithful work is sure. It may be, however, we have wanted results of wishing that needy souls might have life, and that Christ might see the travail of His soul and be satisfied. Have you ever wept for souls?... Have I? 'He that goeth forth and weepeth, bearing precious seed, shall doubtless come again with rejoicing, bringing his sheaves with him.' "

This came to John as a pean of praise, a fore-gleam of the victory which was to be his. For later Praying Hyde had the privilege of asking each year for a certain number of souls during that period and God honored his faith and gave him the number for which he prayed.

When John returned to his village visitation, finding no converts, he called two or three workers together that they might search into the causes for what seemed to be spiritual failure. Writing to the Carthage College magazine he opens his heart to his classmates, saying, "This year there were no conversions in the villages. There were last year. What is the reason? This reason we are seeking... The very thought of seeking was started and confirmed today by mentioning the matter in this letter...

"We are thinking of taking tomorrow just as a day of prayer ... and if we do, I believe it will be fruitful. If our hearts and lives are not right, but become right before God, we shall receive a great blessing; and if it be delayed it will be like holding back a strong-flowing river which will come with mighty power when let go."

John, who had tasted divine love, knew the meaning of prevailing before God. He believed that if his heart was right, God would give him the answer in the form of converts. "It is the essence of love to be thus," he affirms. "If the heart be right blessing cannot be withheld, it can only be delayed; and to delay such blessing means that it should overwhelm us when it does come."

John little realized that he was writing a prophecy which would be ten years in reaching maturity and fulfillment. He was laying up the prayers, storing up soul-faithfulness, banking his labors in heaven, and he knew with the feeling of assurance that the day of rewards would come and the river of divine blessings would break its banks and flood India with refreshings. John was a conquering eagle for the Almighty. His soul was blessed with the anointing of God and laboring thus he awaited the heavenly outpourings in full assurance of faith.

"The life in Christ is a wondrous life," he affirms in the confidence of God's glory, "sometimes an experience of joy that can only be described in the words—'They shall mount up with wings as eagles.' And how the currents of life sweep upward too from the solid rock as in the thick of flying darts one realizes that he stands upon the atonement of Jesus Christ . . . I find the nearer one comes to Jesus Christ the more earnestly he prays the fifty-first Psalm."

It was that Psalm-prayer which John was always repeating after David, who said, "Have mercy upon me . . . Wash me thoroughly . . . and cleanse me . . . Behold I was shapen in iniquity . . . Purge me with hyssop, and I shall be clean: wash me, and I shall be whiter than snow . . . Create in me a clean heart, O God; and renew a right spirit within me . . . Restore unto me the joy of salvation . . . Then will I teach transgressors . . . open thou my lips and my mouth shall show forth thy praise . . . Then shalt thou be pleased with the sacrifices of righteousness.''

This was John Hyde, who no longer could be looked upon as a neophyte, a kingdom apprentice. He had laid the foundations of his missionary endeavors well and wisely. Already during these four years he had entered into his life's work, and from his great love—this village ministry—he was never to depart. Though later he was to visit conferences, churches and districts with his evangelism of prayer, still he in the end was to return to his village visitations and here win his many souls for the Master.

Chapter III

MOLDING THE MAN

God was fashioning Hyde's soul into the pattern which He could use in the kingdom. Only in the crucible of India's seething millions could his life take on the luster of refined gold which the Almighty had determined. There were to be trials, but those trials only drove John to the source of victory, the Throne of Grace. He was to know defeat, but these defeats were to be swallowed up in conquest. Under the lashing of temptations and persecutions his character was to be so toughened that he would later be able to command God.

The next eight years were to produce such results. Many of these years were in seclusion, when both his endeavor and its results were for the eye of God alone. Occasionally he lifts the curtain and unveils what he was doing, but only spasmodically are we so blessed. And when one asks, "What was John doing during those years?" the answer invariably is, "Oh, he was just a village missionary, visiting here and there ... "

But in those "here-and-there years" God was leading John along by the hand quietly into paths of Christian obedience and beauty until in the end he was to receive a new vision of the Christ. Without those hidden years there could have been no Sialkot revival, no Sialkot conventions when the glory of the Lord filled the tent, the buildings, the compound, until it seemed to missionary and Indian alike, "We are walking on holy ground."

On February, 1896, John found time to acknowl-
edge a letter from Martha Gray and the Christian
Endeavor members which he had received nine
months before. " . . . But my long silence might
imply that no answer was to be expected. And yet
I like to answer the letters that reach me for friend-
ship's sake . . . I want the correspondence more than
ever now that if it be possible thereby the prayers
of others might be brought to bear definitely and
powerfully especially upon the work . . . "

This letter is addressed from Chabba village, one
of the places where his tent was occasionally pitched.
Here in the midst of his failures, for this is the year
of no conversions, he feels the need of linking the
prayers of friends to the work of evangelization.

"I believe that missionaries," he goes on to say,
"do a mighty work with the prayers of earnest
Christians round about them. A work carried on
with prayer from hearts right with God must be
successful. As Mr. Moody says, 'If our hearts are
right with God, our prayers must be answered.'

"By the way, that is a wholesome word. It suits
my thought."

It must be remembered that this was the year
of Mott's visit and of the Pentecostal outpourings,
of which he speaks, that swept many into the kingdom.

Continuing, he says, "Much is said and written
these days about 'The Higher Life,' but that word
of Mr. Moody's brings it all down to our common
understanding as that life relates to prayer." Continuing, he refers to an answer given him by Dr.
Ullman as to what constitutes the Holy Spirit's
fullness.

" 'The baptism of the Holy Spirit is a heart for the work.' At the time I thought, 'Can this be all it means?' Possibly that answer might encourage one to rest satisfied with a low intensity of interest . . . but not if he enters into the meaning of the thought. The more I have thought of it the more have I liked the answer. To have a heart constantly for Christ's work is wonderfully blessing."

John adds that he had been at the village two weeks carrying on the Gospel work, and that "the big tent has been sent on to Lauke, a mile away, where we expect to go on Thursday to spend two weeks or so."

We enter into his work when he relates, "I have been here three weeks. A catechist is with me and we go in to our monthly meeting of workers Saturday and Sunday. This is a new arrangement and we hope, yes, fully expect, a blessing from it . . . I have been led into earnest, believing prayer for the coming meeting. We want much that we may have blessings in our district.

"It is good indeed just to put one's self into the hands of the Lord, praying for a definite object, and see how the Lord leads . . . "

He became greatly disturbed in his own mind when he saw the disheartening response to the offer of salvation, and there had been so little Christian results, so he says in the letter, "Prayer for another object which has been running along a good deal in my mind . . . Why are not people this year in these villages as before becoming Christians?"

The press of work made it impossible for him to continue the message, and so he laid it aside until

March 11 when he took up the thread again. He relates how this lack of decisions had been bothering
his spirit, and that for some time there were not the
finest feelings between him and two other workers;
but after much prayer the workers came to him and
the matter was straightened out. He says, "Wasn't
it good?"

The heart of his interest shows through in this
year of no decisions, for he states that while at the
Chabba village he searched his life to find out what
he might ask God for in the coming meetings. "I
determined to ask God to give us one real Israel, a
wrestler with God, a prince prevailing. Paterson
(the speaker at the meeting) joined me in this." It
was at the meetings that John felt he had come
so close to the Lord he could command the
Almighty, such fellowship coming from the passages, "Command ye me," and "Ask what I shall
give thee."

"I believe," he says, "God granted the request.
It was what I would have asked had Jesus been
visibly before me and I did not see how He could
refuse the petition."

It was this quality of coming directly into the
divine presence with his prayer requests which was
to cause India to remember John as "Praying
Hyde." While praying with Paterson John felt that
God granted him this power to be a real Israel, a
prince of requesting, for India. "My heart feels
joyful and at rest about it all," he affirms.

Then he recognizes the greatness of this prayer
burden he is to bear, and analyzing his own weakness, he offers the thought, "But how little I know

of the love and power of our Saviour . . . How my
poor little weak faith struggles and strains to lay
hold of what Christ is so ready and able to grant . . .
There is mighty power in prayer but how little I
know about it and how feeble is my boldness in ap-
proaching Him who uses every means to induce us
to come boldly and prevail.''

He is writing in his little tent, which for a week
or thereabouts has been pitched in the same place.
Later as the heat is intense he hopes to return to
the head station that ''I might get in out of it.'' An
insight into John's character is found in a note
which says that Dr. Newton is coming to the boys'
school a little later, where Hyde himself teaches in
the evenings. ''Last night I played Indian ball with
some of the small boys,'' he says. ''First time I
have, but it gave me a fine opportunity later to speak
of Christ before men and boys.''

The pulsating heart of John breaks through when
he relates that day by day God gave him strength
for the duties, adding, ''I keep in good health,
though the limits of it do not seem far off at any
time.'' In all the work the key to his success is seen
in the fact that he seeks for the leadership of the
Holy Spirit, and there are no tasks too difficult but
he is willing to undertake them.

''I know but one word — *obedience*. I know how
a soldier will obey an order even to death and I
can't expect to look Jesus Christ in the face and
obey Him less than a soldier his commander.''

In trying to keep close to the Indian heart, he
found that he could do so better by mastering the
Bible in the vernacular, which he accomplished not

only by studying it in preparation for his messages
to native audiences but also for his private devo-
tions. The result was a fluency, familiarity and
ease in the use of the Hindustani Bible which made
him master where others were often helpless crip-
ples in its use.

One task in which John had engaged during these
years was teaching the English Bible in the boys'
high school at Ludhiana. This kept him close to the
Indian mind as well as forced him to dig deep into
the sacred pages. But as soon as he was freed of
this he went straight for his village work. Nor was
he content to preach to the natives from afar.

He wanted to be as one of them. "He buried himself with them," says Sarah Wherry, a fellow missionary, "living among them, eating often with
them, and winning to Christ a considerable village
group. Going from village to village, there came to
light conditions which needed cleaning up — men
fallen into sin, quarrels, lapses of Christians back
into idolatry. All of these were heavy burdens upon
John Hyde's spirit and no time was too much to
spend in prayer and patient dealing with those
concerned."

In such times as these he would gather a group
about him, and instead of scolding or lecturing them,
would call on all to pray. Perhaps for two or
three hours he would be on his knees or even on his
face before the natives, mostly in silence. Finally
the group would break down, confess their sins, and
start all over again.

There were cases when his deafness was an asset
as he dealt with such groups, for he could not hear

their restlessness nor the noise when the crowd began to diminish, so absorbed he was in prayer.

In his work conventionalities meant little to him. Dinner hours or times of sleep were forgotten if he could aid a soul in some way. In one boarding house where he stayed for some time, so irregular was his attendance at meals that the hostess said, "In his absence I think how harsh I have been and that I must be forgiving, but when he comes into the house and makes all sorts of demands, I feel worse toward him than ever . . . But on coming back he is so unselfish, so willing to go hungry rather than make any trouble, that I forgive him and go to extra trouble to see that he has what he needs."

One who knew him well during these times says that when Hyde came into a room there was a decided alteration in the atmosphere, for his contagious smile brought a sunshine magic with him. "His coming always furnished a sense of longing for something he had which I wanted, but I did not want to be like him," says Miss Wherry.

In describing differences in personality traits which were used of the Holy Spirit, Hyde said to a fellow missionary, "Personality is a vessel, always individual in contour. So when God's Spirit fills the individual, transforming him into the divine likeness, He does not conform each to a common form or mold."

The year 1897 is broken by a six weeks' vacation at Poona, near Bombay, where he stayed with Robert P. Wilder, whose prayers had brought the Student Volunteer Movement into being at Mt. Hermon where D. L. Moody had invited a group of students to be present for a meeting. "His home is such a holy place," says Hyde, "and he is so sensible and happy, too."

Reporting on the church development of that year, he affirms that "the Christians are taking more interest in the work than I have ever known before. God is blessing individuals among us in Bible study, confession of sin and restitution."

The following was a year of sickness for John, yet while he was laid aside for seven months with typhoid fever, the time was not lost, for he gave himself to prayer and Bible study. Stepping on the heels of the typhoid were two serious abscesses in his back, which brought on a nervousness bordering on a complete breakdown. This compelled him to take a rest cure for some time.

"For a long time after my illness of last May, nervous weakness kept me in the hills, though I wished much to go back to work. I did not leave the hills until December 1. Then I spent a few days in Ludhiana at our Annual Mission Meeting, and a few at Lahore, reaching my home at Ferozepore just before Christmas."

All during the year, he affirms, the prayer of Jabez, recorded in I Chronicles 4:10, kept flooding his soul with its melody. *"Enlarge my borders,"* it sang, day by day, for weeks on end. At length God answered that prayer, John thinks, in the form of his sickness, that he might have time to tune his soul more carefully to the heavenly strains.

"The answer was an illness, straitening and limiting strength and efforts — taking me, keeping me from work for months, pressing home lessons of waiting, impressing the great lesson, 'Not my will but thine be done.' But with the waiting and straitening came spiritual enlargement. How often God withholds the temporal or delays it that we may long for and seek the spiritual.''

During that troublesome year the mission work had also been greatly hampered by lack of funds in the treasury necessary to carry on needed activities. The cut in finances John said was greater that year than ever before. ''Perhaps the lack of funds is due to the lack of prayer to Him who says, 'The silver is mine and the gold is mine.' ''

This fund shortage was a disguised blessing, for the Indian Church put forth a greater effort than before at self-support. There was also a tangible spiritual result, described thus, ''Our whole mission unites in prayer every Sunday for the outpouring of the Holy Spirit upon us.'' And Hyde was to feel the effects of this prayer. After returning to his head station, though he was strong enough for only a week or two to itinerate among the villages, they were days greatly blessed of God.

''The people listened very attentively and many were turned to Christ,'' he says. ''I baptized several and many more were enrolled as catechists.''

He concluded an 1898 letter to American friends with the words, ''Will you not each one seek God's face in prayer for India and for me that my health may be precious in His sight? India is so exhausting, and I do want to stay here.''

The battery of his energy was being discharged faster than he could restore it, and John recognized the danger he faced. Either he must tap the source

of divine health or return to America. God in these
trying times was permitting John's body to weaken
that his soul might be strengthened.

Around the bend of the new year, 1899, Hyde was
to begin mastering the lesson of nights of prayer.
This was in the end to be the source of his spiritual
achievement, when through the dark nights his soul
would be alone with God, listening, beseeching, com-
manding the Almighty. The process was not an easy
one to master.

His letter of that year to the Carthage College
magazine tells the story of a divine transformation
going on in his prayer life.

"The years have been full of trial which tells
even on physical power, and I have not known how
to work below my capacity to withstand and endure.
The spiritual things of India have been intense in
my soul, and my body is not trained to bear strain
easily."

During the past year he relates that he was in
Ferozepore, and though not well, he was until
March, 1899, trying to recover somewhat from the
strain of the winter's sickness.

"It has been one of work and prayer. Results I
have not seen, or but little. There are a few inquirers
and our work has seen a few baptisms. I am a helper
of Dr. Newton and his family, and want, as Meyer
says, to help my Heavenly Father a little in His
work. I have felt led to pray for others this year
as never before. I never before knew what it was
*to work all day and then pray all night before God
for another.*

"Early in the morning, four or five o'clock, or
even earlier, and late at night to twelve or one

o'clock. In college or at parties at home, I used to keep such hours for myself or pleasure, and can I not do as much for God and souls?"

It was here that Hyde learned the lesson of nights of prevailing prayer which in the end were to become the rule of his Christian experience. He knew the meaning of the sacrifice of time and self for the cause of intercession, and though results now were few, the day was coming when they would be numerous.

During the year of 1900 Hyde continued living with Dr. Newton and his family at Ferozepore, and remarks, "It is not a small privilege to live in a saintly home." Not being honored with a home of his own, he enjoyed the sacred blessings of another's. John was never to know the joy of married bliss, remaining a bachelor that he might thereby the better serve his Master.

The year 1901 was marked with spiritual increase in the village where he lived as well as elsewhere. "We have used the Word and prayed much and worked earnestly, and several evils have been removed . . . It makes one believe in a living, present Saviour, to see His people blessed in answer to definite prayer, and inquirers, though only a few, asking to be taught, when our condition is so weak in every way."

Wondering how the century began with his American friends, he says, "I believe it is to be a time of Pentecostal power, or even a double portion of the Pentecostal Spirit. I interpret God as laying a burden of prayer on souls, pouring out the spirit of grace and supplication that Christians and the un-

converted may look on Him . . . and mourn in deep
contrition of sin . . .

"We live in the latter age. Can we not have a
century besides the first which has the normal life
of its own age? I hail in the twentieth century, the
blessing of our age restored — a Church holy in life,
triumphant in faith, self-sacrificing in service with
one aim, to preach Christ crucified 'unto the uttermost part of the earth.' "

Realizing that the Pentecostal power would follow
only Pentecostal methods, he tried to urge upon his
homeland friends the necessity of awakening to
prayer's power.

"And if this blessing begins with the deadness in
the Church and an eclipse of faith . . . it cannot be
worse than in the days preceding Pentecost. The
disciples were then shut up to prayer, and can anyone say what would happen now if God's Church
should give herself up to this same resource?"

This was Hyde's growing burden. He felt the
consuming need of prayer as the foundation of
spiritual results in India no less than in America.
In his work this passion took the form of constant
seasons of prayer that Christ might visit his adopted
country with a mighty revival.

Weak in body, he felt the need of a furlough from
his heavy labors, and so he visited his homeland in
1902, ten years after having set sail for India. There
were many changes, the greatest of which was the
absence of his dear father from the Carthage church
where he had preached so diligently and so long.

He traveled as much as his money would permit
and writes to a friend, "I am poor and needy, yet
the Lord thinketh upon me." He visited his rela-

tives and enjoyed the fellowship. Upon his return home he recognized a distinct uplifting of the foreign missionary standard of enthusiasm and concern.

Wherever he spoke the burden of his message was the fullness of the Spirit as the necessary energy for missionary endeavors. "In this is the power needed," he said. " 'Ye shall receive power after that the Holy Ghost is come upon you,' and then indeed shall the Church witness at home and unto the uttermost parts of the earth."

Returning to India he took up his village work with a new zest as his energies were higher after the rest in America. Looking about him he saw the whitened harvest, the scarcity of laborers, and said, "We need many missionaries and your prayers for laborers, both foreign and Indian. We are here in this district alone, two men and three ladies in 950,-000 people."

That year, 1904, was to mark the changing point in Hyde's life, and was to see the transformation of the ordinary missionary into Praying Hyde, an achiever for God. At the break of the year he recognized the change, saying:

"This year has been different from others to me. For ten years after coming to India, I was 'running' and did not 'grow weary.' But the past year I have been feeling the drudgery and homesickness of life here. In the midst of this, to 'keep a-pluggin' away' in patience and sweetness and courage and quiet with a strong heart for the work — this I think is the finest quality we may have in Christian service."

The year began inauspiciously, except for the fact that John's strength was again at a low ebb, but before spring was over a new touch was to be received which again showed him in truth, "It is not by might nor by power, but by my Spirit, saith the Lord."

Chapter IV

UNITED FOR PRAYER

Hyde was now at the fulfillment of those long years of prayer. God had tutored him in the school of intercession and at last it was time for visible results to appear as the fruitage of those nights spent on his face before the Almighty. In prayer unity there is spiritual strength, and God was to use John Hyde as the rallying center around which the missionaries were to pivot their petitions.

The spark had already been kindled at Sialkot, the headquarters of the United Presbyterian Mission, which had been in operation for almost a half century. Here were buildings and accommodations suited for a great crowd — though not so large a gathering as God soon precipitated upon them.

In the girls' school, headed by Mary Campbell and an assistant, a spirit of revival broke out early in 1904, which produced a decided spiritual upheaval among the girls, many of whom had made public confession of their sins and had been gloriously born again.

This revival spirit spread to the near-by theological seminary where a high tide of spiritual bliss marked the native theological students. Two of these students, Sabhu Mall and Mallu Chand, decided to visit the boys' school which was three miles distant. But on arriving they had not been permitted to speak to the lads about their souls. Those in charge had become nervous at the appearance of what they termed emotionalism in religion, which in reality was but the working of the Holy Spirit in salvation.

Returning to the girls' school where they met Miss Campbell the seminarians told her about their rebuke. Before leaving that night for their own rooms Sabhu led in prayer and definitely asked God for an outpouring upon the school.

"Oh, Lord, please grant that the place we were forbidden to speak tonight," he said in prayer, "may become the center from which great blessings shall flow to all parts of India."

That prayer was soon to be answered, for shortly Dr. W. B. Anderson was placed in charge of the boys' work, and feeling concerned for a spiritual outburst he called others to gather at Sialkot for prayer. The call went out for a meeting in April, 1904, for prayer warriors to gather that they might prevail before God for India.

John Hyde was a leading spirit in this call and the following movement. Among those invited was the Rev. McCheyne Paterson, Mrs. Alice McClure and others. When the group came together there were not many of them, but they united their petitions. All the members of the band were greatly inspired by Hyde's prayer habits. At this first meeting was laid the foundation for the Punjab Prayer Union which was to exert a tremendous influence upon India's spiritual life, as well as be the forerunner of the Sialkot conventions.

Those becoming members were asked to sign a list of principles in the form of questions.

"1. Are you praying for quickening in your own life, in the life of your fellow workers, and in the Church?

"2. Are you longing for greater power of the Holy Spirit in your own life and work, and are you convinced that you cannot go on without this power?

"3. Will you pray that you may not be ashamed of Jesus?

"4. Do you believe that prayer is the great means for securing this spiritual awakening?

"5. Will you set apart one-half hour each day as soon after noon as possible to pray for this awakening, and are you willing to pray *till the awakening comes?*"

From the beginning Hyde was an integral part of this Union, devoting his unbounding prayer energies to the cause it represented. Lifting up his eyes, he saw as always India's white fields and he knew the only method by which harvesters could be made available was by that which his old father had taught him when they gathered around the family altar. So he began praying — by the day, throughout the night, days and nights together, until God heard and an awakening came.

When Hyde, with his two friends, McCheyne Paterson and George Turner, began to pray, as is always the case, God began to answer. Revivals have never been the product of the spontaneous combustion of spiritual forces; rather they have been paid for by prayer. Finney's revivals came about because Father Nash lay on his face in prayer while the evangelist brought the message. So now in Hyde's life as the revival was about to dawn, these men, with others, were paying the purchase price.

As a result of the meeting of this Punjab Prayer Union, there was issued a general call throughout India for all Christian workers to gather at Sialkot for a Christian life convention. The news was broadcast, and the Christian Training Institute of the United Presbyterian Mission at Sialkot was to act as host to the group.

The meeting was set for late August, but that there might be no spiritual dearth John Hyde and Paterson prayed for thirty days and nights before the convention opened. On the tenth day Turner joined the friends, so that for twenty-one days and nights the Throne of God was bombarded by the prayer ammunition of three men, men who had long ago consecrated themselves to the task of bringing spiritual life to sin-deadened souls.

And Hyde was no stranger to this day-and-night praying. For many years he had practiced it diligently. The record of those thirty-one days and nights of prayer is closed in the Book of Heaven, for no word of them has ever seeped through to the outside. Those sainted prayer warriors were not on dress parade. They went forth to battle with their only weapon with as much earnestness as soldiers in any king's army.

Hyde wanted no spiritual miscarriage when the convention met. Plans had been carefully laid for entertainment, and at the North Compound the group was to assemble. Little did John realize that he was there starting a movement which would spread throughout India and help to establish a spiritual life convention which exists today as a power in Punjab.

From that first convention until today, thirty-eight years later, with but one or two exceptions when the ravages of cholera made meeting impossible, the convention has poured forth into India streams of Christian power.

Hyde's first concern for the meeting was that the spirit of prayer should run high, and so he gave himself to the ministry of intercession continually. There were two prayer rooms, one for women and one for men, and after the first day of the 1904 convention until the end the prayer rooms were never vacant. Usually John was one of those who remained. there constantly.

One of the Indian ministers, seeing John carry this heavy burden, remarked, "When I see this man from another country so burdened for my people, I feel ashamed when I think how little I am doing for my own flesh and blood."

Among the Indians themselves John found many who joined him in the prayer room, including eighty-year-old Kanaya who spent three of the ten nights in prayer. This man was marvelously used of God in scattering the holy fire wherever he went.

The change in Hyde's spiritual life was so visible from the start that fellow missionaries could not understand it. At the meeting, while John was speaking on the Holy Spirit, God opened to him the plan of sanctification by faith, and such a touch of God and light from heaven came upon him that at the close of the convention he remarked to friends, among whom was Hervey Griswold, author of *Insight into Hinduism*, "I must not lose this vision."

Nor did from that time on the vision depart from him, but grew rather the brighter and more scintillant. With the vision came a decided quickening of mental powers and an insight into the Bible which he had not before possessed. Later while John was speaking at the annual meeting of the Punjab Presbyterian Mission a veteran missionary who heard his series of addresses said, "Where did he get those ideas? He never had them before."

The answer must be found in the prayer room at Sialkot. Prayer to Hyde, from then on was meditation, communion with a Friend. From that first convention on through until his last, he virtually never slept, spending his time in the prayer room. "These seasons of prayer were for John Hyde," says Griswold, "not only emotionally satisfying and intellectually quickening, but also volitionally bracing and creative." From these prayer sessions he went into evangelistic action for God.

That prayer room was not only for Hyde a place of communion but also for others it was a place of spiritual quest. While in the prayer room he was usually surrounded by Indians who were seeking Christ. This henceforth was to be a distinguishing mark. Wherever he was found he was surrounded with natives whom he was pointing to Christ.

Mary Campbell tells how, when he left the prayer room, she saw Hyde immediately surrounded by natives and shortly many of them were on their faces seeking salvation, for John's spirit was so charged with God that they were drawn to him and through him led to the Master.

During the first ten or twelve years of his missionary service he was slow of speech, feeling his way with caution, but after the first Sialkot convention there was a noticeable quickening of his mental powers, revealed in public address as well as in his private conversation. He was as a man whose tongue once bound was now suddenly released, and out of him gushed streams of life-giving words.

John had come to the convention to lead Bible studies during the morning, and when called upon to speak it was as though suddenly he had been immersed in the length and breadth and height and depth of the love of God.

Many unusual stories are told of his reactions in public. One evening he had been asked to speak to the men in the compound tabernacle while the women were holding forth in a missionary bungalow. When the meeting time came the men were seated on mats, but Hyde did not appear. Singing started, and after several hymns at length he came in.

Sitting on a mat in front of the group, he remained silent for some time. Then he arose and said:

"Brothers, I did not sleep any last night, and I have not eaten anything today. I have been having a controversy with God. I feel that He has warned me to come here and testify to you concerning some things that He has done for me, and I have been arguing with Him that I should not do this. Only this evening a little while ago I got peace concerning the matter and have agreed to obey Him, and now I have come to tell you just some things that He has done for me."

Then he unburdened his heart, confessing what God had wrought in him, and told some of the conflicts he formerly had with sin. Finishing with a note of victory, he said, "Let us have a season of prayer."

Remarks one who attended that service, "I remember how the little company prostrated themselves on the mats on their faces in the Oriental manner, and then how for a long time, how long I do not know, man after man rose to his feet to pray, how there was such a confession of sin as most of us had never heard before, and such crying for mercy and help."

The gathering disbanded very late that night, but many lives had been magnificently transformed for God through the service.

It was during this first convention that Hyde arose in a public gathering with both men and women present and opened the casket of his buried past, revealing the ugliest of sins which had marked his early life. Though they had been covered by Christ's blood, still John said he felt they should be confessed. This was after he had spent nights in the prayer room. Many present bowed their heads as the stories of iniquity were revealed. They were so ashamed to hear such confessions that many of them left the room.

Mary Campbell told the writer recently, looking back to that meeting, "As John Hyde arose and began his public confession I thought it was out of place. I was so ashamed that I bowed my head, and thought of leaving the meeting. I was called from that first convention before it was over. So I was very glad to be out from under the thing.'' When upon returning she found the Holy Spirit in action and felt the blessed atmosphere, she recognized that the confession was of God.

The confessional tide was on and one by one people arose in those early meetings and laid bare their sins to public gaze. Older ministers looked with horror upon what was happening, but as spiritual results began to unfold they each recognized their mistake and declared the work to be of God.

With confession came conviction, and accompanying conviction was salvation. One native evangelist became very vexed because his grown daughter had confessed to sin in her life, and he came to the meeting to speak against what was going on. But when he saw the crowd in tears and sensed the presence of God, he also became convicted for unbelief, and tearfully sought his way to the cross, where he too joined the host of the redeemed.

There was no gauge for Hyde's actions during those conventional meetings. Once when he was to be the speaker at a prayer service, he did not arrive, even though he was known to be on the grounds. When the hour had passed he finally appeared, his face radiant and his step light, saying, ''I had no message, and I knew the Lord could use someone else or speak to you in His own way.''

Said a missionary present at the service, ''At first I thought Hyde was acting peculiar, or was a little unbalanced, but as I watched him and saw the visible results which followed, I realized he was following the Spirit's leadership. And in it all God was present.''

"It may be that I have been telling you more of the Sialkot convention," writes Emma Norris, a fellow worker in India with Hyde, in a personal letter to the author, "than I have of John Hyde. But the two are so inextricably bound up together that it is hard to separate them. Whether in the prayer room, where he spent most of his time during the convention, or in the meetings or on the grounds, singing or speaking, modest and unobtrusive though he was, there was something that made you realize his identity with the thing, the purpose, the deep reality of what the convention stood for."

So powerful were the effects of John's confessions that he was led to repeat them in many gatherings. "Sometimes one felt them an obsession," says a friend, but when the results of his acts became known, all recognized the holiness of Hyde's inner man as well as his outward cleanness.

So great was his utter release from ordinary duties so he might gain time for prayer that Dr. Ullman, his first language teacher, said, "Hyde, the thing you need is naked faith," meaning of course that Hyde was in danger of substituting the length of his prayers for the believing strength of them. John recognized this and thanked his former teacher for the admonition.

After the meetings there were often all-night rejoicing parties when Hyde along with others forgot their dignity and marched round the tent singing, shouting and throwing their hats into the air. They clapped their hands and rejoiced in the Lord.

"And I sat in my room," says Emma Norris thirty-six years later, as she recalls the glory of that scene, "and my heart rebelled against such undignified behavior. My heart not attuned to my head cried out for the joy that could make people forget themselves. But the rebellion was stronger than the hunger, and at length however hunger won and I became content in the group."

However great the public demonstrations, the real secret of the convention was to be found in the prayer rooms. When the tide ran high, missionaries and others brought their friends into the rooms that they might be converted, and in these rooms was such a sense of power that confession and belief were easy.

A young missionary with but a year's service to his credit was attending the convention when he said to Pengwern Jones, a close friend of Hyde, that he did not feel at home in the services, not being accustomed to such a sense of the divine nearness. Two or three days later after he too had visited the prayer room, he returned, his face aglow saying, "Do you know, I have found out the secret of this convention — *it is the prayer room.* I never saw anything like it."

And Jones in his memories of Hyde as published in *Praying Hyde* adds, "I told him that I quite agreed with him, and we had a chat over the blessings that he had received and the new visions of Christ he had. This prayer room . . . was the work of the Holy Spirit through Hyde; it was he that spent the first nights on the watchtower, but joined almost from the first by his friend and beloved brother McCheyne Paterson."

Jones once asked Hyde how he had learned the lesson of nights of prayer which so vitalized his convention work. Hyde replied, "Some time ago I was asked to speak at a Bible school one morning, and had no time for preparation. So I remained up all night to prepare the message. The next day I thought that since I had spent a night in getting the message ready, there was need of getting myself ready also. And would not a night of prayer and praise be a good preparation for a real blessing the following day? This was the Holy Spirit's suggestion, and I remained in prayer that whole night. Enjoying it so much, I repeated it the following night."

It was this that gave birth to his practice of nights of prayer. Soon he found friends willing to join him and from these united prayer sessions came the Sialkot prayer rooms.

During the convention, Hyde's bed was placed between that of Pengwern Jones and Dr. Griswold. On retiring Jones noticed one particular night that Hyde's bed had not been used at all, for he had been spending his time in the prayer room.

"But one morning," says Jones, "he rushed in and went down on his knees by the bedside. This was in the early morning soon after dawn. I went to the *chota-hazri* (early breakfast) and came back and found him still praying. Then I went out to the prayer meeting and morning service, and came back about eleven o'clock, and found him still praying."

After going to the 12:30 breakfast, as the Indians call it, Jones returned to his cot where he lay down for rest. During the time he watched Hyde, who had not moved from his knees. In the afternoon Jones attended the service, returning each time to the sleeping-room to see what Hyde was doing.

"At six o'clock he was still on his knees, and had been all day. As I had an hour to wait until dinner, I determined to watch him and if he arose from his knees, I would ask him how it was possible for him to remain quiet the whole day and to pray while there was so much noise around, for people were coming in and going out the whole time . . .

"In half an hour or so he looked up and smiled. I sat on his bed and asked what was the secret of all this. I also asked him to allow me to fetch a cup of tea, but he refused the tea, asking for water only."

With his face illuminated Hyde looked at his friend and exclaimed, "Let me tell you, what a vision I had — a new vision of Christ."

Life radiant, heart joyous, he had come into the living presence of Christ and was thus freshly under the glow of that heavenly touch. Jones says, "I shall never forget his words as they gave me a new vision of Christ . . . I could not keep the tears back. At times I felt that it could not be true, that Christ had never suffered so much for me . . . How I wish I could repeat it as Hyde brought me step by step to see Christ that evening."

In the course of the revelation Hyde showed three things he had seen in the spiritual illumination of his own soul under the presence of Christ's glory. He saw how Christ had become a man, emptying Himself and leaving the glory world that He might enter a sinful world. The cost, John said, was great for He lived in an atmosphere of sin.

"And it was no wonder," he said, "that Christ often escaped from the haunts of men, from the depressing, suffocating odor of sin to the mountains to have a breath of fresh air of heaven."

While Hyde was delivering the vision, as it had been vividly painted on the screen of his own mind, Jones listened, head bowed, to the story. "I felt that even the Incarnation was an Infinite Sacrifice, even if the death on Calvary had never taken place."

Hyde stopped and said, "And He took this place — became man — for me."

Describing the second phase of his vision, John said he had seen Christ as *He became a slave.* Time and again in depicting the story of a slave's life in the East, Hyde added, *"for me, for me!"* To John the sacrifice had become personalized. Sobs broke the narrative as he unrolled the canvas of memory and showed Christ to Jones. Together they wept for a long time at the thought of Christ's suffering.

"I saw more," Hyde took up the strain again. "I saw that my Jesus became a dog, a pariah dog, *for me.* This was too awful to think of, but when I thought of His life, I had come to the conclusion that the life of Christ had more of the characteristics of a dog's life than anything else, and this I have been doing, worshiping Him and praising Him for it."

Gradually Hyde pointed out the similarity of Christ's life to that of an Eastern outcast dog: neither of them had a place to lay their heads; both received the kicks and blows of men.

"Shall I ever forget the tenderness of Hyde as he spoke of the sufferings of Christ? I remember nothing of the dinner that night; my impression is that we both sat on that bed for hours, speaking of Christ. I shall never forget it, nor the vision I had of the love of Christ, going lower and lower, suffering more and more, and *all for me.*" Jones too had entered into that vision of the Master as Hyde told him of it.

Is there any reason why Hyde should not say at the close of that convention, "Oh, I must not lose this blessing. I must not lose this vision"?

He had glimpsed Christ through prayer, and walking into heaven's full-orbed light he could never remain the same. But he must not live on that Mount of Transfiguration, for down in India's valleys there were multitudes waiting for the healing touch which his life would bring.

CHAPTER V

FORWARD THROUGH PRAYER

John Hyde at that first Sialkot convention laid the foundation for greater things in the coming years and at the future conventions which were to assemble up to two thousand Christian leaders of the nation. Little is known of Hyde's work during 1904 following the conference, save that he returned to his mission duties.

Laboring so many years in the villages with native helpers, he conceived of a training school for village workers. He saw the vision of the need, and it was necessary for him to finance it out of his own salary, for there were no available funds for this new venture.

He graced the new institution, which in reality was but a small gathering of his helpers in the off-hot or rainy seasons when they could not be working elsewhere, with the name of "The School of the Minor Prophets." It was necessary not only for John to finance the school but to conduct it as well, save as he was able to prevail upon busy mission-aries to give him a mental lift with the instruction.

Little did he realize when his Minor Prophet school came into being, brewed in his own mind which was aflame with holy passion for village evangelization, that he was laying the foundation for an important phase of India's educational work. The school was later moved to Moga and furnished the seed out of which the Moga Training School for

Village Workers was to come. This institution through the years has meant much to the educational life of India, and without Hyde it would have not been possible.

John's prayer room at the old dispensary and the bridge at Moga under which he used to pray are still pointed out to visitors.

During the remainder of 1904 and the following summer evidences of the Sialkot revival were appearing in many places. Prayer conferences and "prayer fires" were scattered wherever the workers lived who had attended the Sialkot convention. And in these prayer places and meetings souls were gradually being led into the glow of redemption's light.

In the United Presbyterian summer Bible schools and at other meetings were evidences of God's workings. Early in the year prayer was started for the 1905 convention. It was the heartfelt desire of all that this convention should surpass the previous meeting.

Word of the coming spiritual retreat was broadcasted throughout India. This was scheduled for August 25 to September 3, 1905. Dr. Pengwern Jones, a Spirit-filled missionary of the Kasri Hill Mission, was invited to begin the convention with an address. Arising, he faced an audience of several hundred, and spoke on the subject, "Can God Trust You?"

"The audience was swayed," writes Emma Anderson who was present, "by the power of the Spirit working through him. Time came to close the meeting but in place of its closing the whole congregation was swept onto its face before God. Many cried for

mercy and forgiveness. Often several people would
be praying at the same time. Awful sin was confessed and one felt like covering the ears that one
might not hear. God forgave sin and covered it so
one could not remember afterward much that had
been said."

The revival was on and many souls were born
anew that night. Missionaries who until then had
been accounted "good missionaries," from then on
became *powerful* missionaries. All night long the
hall remained full of people praying and praising
God for His goodness. "I can testify to the fact,"
says Miss Anderson, "that our mission and church
(the United Presbyterian at Sialkot) have been
different ever since that night when God so graciously poured His Spirit upon His people . . . Here
revival fire started in many a heart and is still
burning."

Outlining the source of that peculiar power Miss
Anderson says in *In the Shadow of the Himalayas,*
which she wrote with Mary Campbell:

"The secret of the whole movement lies in the
fact that the convention was conceived in prayer
and prayer has ever had a large place in all the
meetings and management. The prayer rooms are
places of power. Things that have transpired in
those rooms are too sacred to be talked about, too
holy to be touched. They were offerings placed upon
God's altar and must remain there."

A program had been carefully prepared for that
1905 convention. A series of morning meetings was
to have been conducted around the theme of the
Holy Spirit, with Hyde as the principal speaker.
Only one address was delivered. "After that, He

came Himself in great power, and all learned of Him,'' says the mission report of the convention to the homeland board.

Hyde's messages were to have been the main attraction at the Holy Ghost rallies. He had been praying diligently since the Punjab Prayer Union meeting in April for the outpouring of the Holy Spirit in mighty sin-destroying power. As usual the entire nights of prayer did more to prepare the speaker than the message. Often he had fasted until body strength ebbed at low tide. Of that meeting of the Union one writer says, ''God laid upon our hearts the burden of a world plunged in sin. We were permitted to share to some extent in the sufferings of Christ. It was a glorious preparation for the convention.''

During those preparatory prayer sessions God had burned upon the walls of John's mind the command, ''I have set watchmen upon thy walls, O Jerusalem, which shall never hold their peace day nor night; ye that make mention of the Lord, keep not silence, and give him no rest, till he make Jerusalem a praise in the earth'' (Isa. 62:6, 7).

That was John's personal message from God for his own actions in the prayer room. The first night he with others met for their usual all-night session of waiting on God, and they were moved as the shouts and rejoicings of those who were in the meeting broke upon their souls.

God sustained Hyde in these long vigils without sleep, and one remarked on meeting him, ''One could see from his face that it was the presence of Christ that strengthened his weak body.''

When that first morning meeting came John walked quietly in and said, "I thank God, He has given me no message for you today." The audience looked surprised at this, for they were expecting a life-challenging sermon on the Holy Spirit.

The chairman calmly said, "The Holy Spirit is leader of this meeting." The people began to speak as they were moved by the Holy Spirit, and there was liberty but not license. Conviction of sin came over the people like a tidal wave. Many were in great mental agony and intense physical strain as they felt the near presence of God settle upon the congregation. Men and women forgot each other as the divine searchlight was flashed upon their lives. Some began to confess sins which blazed in their hearts, and others, as they arose to speak, trembled as hidden sins were brought to light.

"After this the cloud seemed to lift," says the annual report, "and the sunshine came and flooded the place, and joy was depicted on many countenances. Mouths were filled with laughter and song. Then it was that we began to realize what it is 'to joy in the Holy Ghost.'"

It was this leadership of the Holy Spirit for which Hyde had been praying since the April meeting of the Prayer Union. He had called upon God to reveal Himself and to conceal the speaker. He focused his addresses — what few there were to be during those ten days — on the thought of the immediate appearances of the Spirit.

Weeks earlier the Spirit had attended the Prayer Union meetings of which McCheyne Paterson says, "There was a general breakdown of all hearts when this subject was talked and prayed about. To many the Lamb of God appeared with His wounded hands and side, and showed them how His heart was still made to bleed by His children when they were not fully consecrated to Him, and when they were not filled to overflowing with His Spirit. Little wonder that the convention of 1905 touched so deeply the life of the Punjab Church.''

It was here that John Hyde was at his best as a leader, moved by the power of the Holy Spirit. The mantle of Dr. Lytle of the American Presbyterian Mission had fallen on him. For this missionary had declared the full Gospel of the Spirit's ministry as it was in apostolic times, and had said that when the Spirit filled the Indian Church it would be self-supporting as the Apostolic Church was.

The truth of this assertion is abundantly evidenced by the fact that shortly after the Sialkot conventions began, the mission church of that station assumed its own self-support to a large extent. And those who write the history of the Sialkot group affirm that from the time of the Holy Spirit's coming in 1905 the matter of local self-support increased.

When Hyde did arise to speak at length in the convention of that year, the burden of his message was the infilling of the Holy Spirit. ''How plainly he showed that the Holy Spirit was the One True Witness — to be put first and foremost by all Christians — so that they might also give their witness in His strength and by His help. When he addressed pastors, asking them who was first and foremost in their pulpits, they themselves or the Divine Teacher and Guide into all truth, I do not believe there was

a single preacher who was not convicted of this sin,''
says Paterson.

When Hyde had spoken on the life of Christ, and
life through Christ, tracing the Master's earthly
career, he called upon all present to see that this
life was the result of the Spirit's guidance. Finishing the message of the Holy Spirit in Christ's life,
he was through, and indicated he had no more messages to deliver.

At the beginning of the 1905 convention a group
of dissatisfied people had come to the committee in
whose hands the program arrangements were placed
and asked that the freedom of the previous convention be eliminated. They proposed to do this by so
planning the meetings that there would be little lee-
way for emotional play or the Spirit's upcroppings.

But as soon as the first message was over and
speaker Jones had finished, the committee threw
away its outlined arrangements of topics and speakers. So that the Holy Spirit might have an opportunity to break in upon the people in His own way,
the committee did not ask speakers to appear until
just before meeting time. Thus there were no announced preachers or messages.

John Hyde was asked to be the speaker at an evening meeting. Somehow the word was noised around
and the people said, ''Mr. Hyde will speak tonight.''
The meeting was on and the congregation large, the
chairman was in his accustomed place, and the music
was nearing its end.

Hyde was on the rear of the platform deep in
prayer. On his heart was a message about Christ's
sufferings. Suddenly the congregation sang the
twenty-second Psalm. When the singing was finished

Hyde remained in prayer and the leader read Zechariah 13, commenting on, "What are these wounds between my hands?" He spoke at length on Christ's sufferings for His people and urged that Spirit-baptized Christians be witnesses to the power of the Lord.

Still John was lost in prayer and remained in his seat. Finally the chairman, during the singing of another song, walked to John and placed his hands on his shoulders. "If God has a message for you to give, will you give it now?" he asked.

As Hyde did not stir, John Forman, general chairman of the convention, asked the leader, "Is he going to speak?"

"I have asked him," was the reply. "You ask him too if you are led to do it."

Forman instead arose and proceeded to speak, asking permission to give two messages which God had laid on his heart. The meeting swept through to victory, to be followed by a glorious after-service when souls found the Lord. During this after-meeting John arose from his chair and walked to the prayer room without saying a word to the meeting.

Later when asked about that evening, Hyde said, "I was full of the subject, 'The Glory of Christ's Kingdom,' until the leader pressed my shoulder, and this seemed to crush down upon me. And I began to doubt whether or not I had the message for the meeting." John had learned the needed lesson that he should not speak at a meeting unless he had a direct spiritual leading to do so.

It required a man who lived close to the Lord to be able thus to catch the faintest breathings of the Spirit. Said a friend after the revival was far past,

"We ought to have emphasized the lesson of obedience more than we did. I believe it was want of obedience that grieved the Holy Spirit and stopped that revival."

Men recognized that Hyde was obedient to the Holy Spirit. When those hundreds were gathered they permitted him to assume whatever form of spiritual leadership he desired. Canon Haslam, speaking at the Founders' Week Conference, of the Moody Bible Institute in Chicago, 1941, delivered an address on "Praying Hyde as I Knew Him." He knew Hyde well back in those India days, having first met him at Forman Christian College and later they attended conferences together.

"To Hyde it was revealed," says the Canon, "that the Church had no power because of sin which had not been cleansed from her life; and that sin is washed away only when there is true repentance and confession. He was a part of that Church. Burdened with this thought, after an all-night vigil and a day of fasting and prayer, he came into the presence of a large group of Indian Christian men and spoke openly . . . of his personal conflict with secret sin that was ofttimes repeated, and of how God had led him through to victory. The effect of this open confession was electric."

The Canon says that though he was not present at the time, still on hearing of it he was prepared with many arguments against such open confessions, but on seeing Hyde this objection was wiped away.

"Later I attended a meeting of men," he relates, "where there was a great unburdening of hearts, hearts sin-stricken and broken, followed immediately by the sense and joy of forgiveness. I never was at a holier gathering in my life. I was silenced. God's message to me was, 'Hands off the ark of God.' "

It was for this reason that Hyde was free in the conventions. Another evening Mary Campbell relates how she sat in the audience waiting for Hyde to appear with the message. They had waited for some time but still John continued walking outside the large tent where they were seated.

"I saw him walking out there, and thought really there must be something wrong with his head," she relates. "But when the glory did fall and the meeting was under way I recognized this as the leadership of the Holy Spirit."

Often during these conventions Hyde and Paterson, after praying all night, would spend the day in fasting. When someone asked Hyde to eat, he replied, "I have meat to eat that ye know not of," as the Master before him had said.

Hyde was so careful to obey the Spirit that after his first message on the Scriptures, "Tarry ... until ye be endued with power from on high" (Luke 24:49), and "Be filled with the Spirit" (Eph. 5:18), he refused to speak again until the congregation had sought the baptism of the Holy Spirit.

"Though fully prepared to follow with other addresses it was laid on his heart that these must not be given until the challenge of the first address was fully accepted and the Holy Spirit had been given His rightful place in the lives of those who had heard. For two days he came before the convention, stating that he was not allowed to give further addresses and calling them to remain silent," says Canon Haslam.

This obedience to the Holy Spirit fully altered
Hyde's missionary activities. From then on he was
to learn it was the Spirit's will that he move about
less from village to village but remain at one place
until the divine work was accomplished. He felt he
must not leave without a convert and without definite
baptisms and decisions for Christ. By this means
he formed the nucleus of a church, which would become a witnessing group.

"His method was criticized," says the Canon,
"but one of his severest critics told me, after Mr.
Hyde's death, that of all the churches in their mission, the church at Moga, numbering more than a
thousand, was the strongest spiritually and in the
matter of witnessing and giving of its substance for
evangelism."

Hyde's life in these meetings as always was perfectly surrendered to God, and the results were to
be left to the divine reckoning.

Of course there were to be critics, for many were
not so spiritually tuned to the heavenly anthem, but
for every critic there were hundreds of believers
who had been transformed through the Spirit's work
under Hyde's ministry.

During this 1905 convention sins of a shocking
nature were revealed, which stirred up a great deal
of dissension. A number of native Christian and
American workers decided that they would discuss
the matter with the committee. When the troublesome objections were presented the committee replied, "Let us meet together to pray over the
matter."

The objectors were unwilling to do this, saying
that it was useless to pray until the question had

been decided. Paterson, hearing of the arguments, listened to both sides, saying nothing. One young fellow thumped on the table and shouted, "I'll smash the whole convention."

When Paterson approached Hyde with the story, he listened intently and then replied, "It was not the committee which called for the confessions, but it was the Spirit of God that had moved men to confess. It is impossible to legislate on matters like this. Setting apart meetings for confessions would be taking the matter out of the Spirit's control. The spirit of immorality is prevalent among the Christian professors, and the Spirit sees that extreme measures are needed to get men to realize the sin."

Hyde laid his finger on the source of trouble when he remarked, "Some men I fear are guilty and are afraid that the Holy Spirit will compel them to confess."

When the committee was free to make an expression on the matter they indicated their desire for the Spirit's supreme leadership in the meetings, whatever form it might take.

The annual report to the United Presbyterian Board notes several cases which arose that year. A young man of the mission had committed sin and was afraid that it would be discovered. So heavy was his heart that he left the convention and returned to his home forty miles distant, where he made restitution to the one wronged, coming again to Sialkot to be gloriously transformed. An aged minister's daughter had confessed to serious sins in the public meeting, and her father, a respected worker, became angry about it. He left the meetings and stayed away for some time, to find when he returned that the missionaries wanted him to settle the matter in the prayer room.

Finally he entered, fell on his face, began weeping and cried out, "I have sinned. O God, have mercy on me!" Soon the war clouds rolled away and victory burst upon his life.

"The last Sabbath morning's service," says the report, "was most impressive. There was no sermon, there was no leader. The songs of Zion filled hearts with joy, and they alone could give an outlet to the exuberance of joy felt by so many hearts. Someone announced the thirtieth Psalm. It was sung throughout. An aged minister said, 'Let us sing it again.' And once more this was done, and even the third time it was sung through. This time some shouted for joy, and others like David danced before the Lord as they sang,

"And now to joyous dancing
My sorrow thou hast turned."

The 148th Psalm will long be remembered as the convention song. It was sung day and night. Nothing else could satisfy the souls that were hungry to praise God for all that was in them, and that was round about them."

During this convention two young ministers felt the call of God to go back home and begin the life of self-supporting pastors.

"This they have done and God is blessing them and their people," continues the report. "One returned to his village, and that night held an all-night prayer meeting with his people. A revival began there, and that whole district has been changed by the power of God's Spirit so graciously given in Sialkot. Not only this one district, but many others; not only our own mission, but the whole Punjab, and praise God, the whole of India, are being touched with the Pentecostal flame.''

A picture is drawn of the last service, held about dawn on the morning following the close of the convention. In the courtyard a group of earnest men gathered around a crimson flag on which shone a cross of gold. A native minister conducted a short service, and said, ''We are now soldiers going forth to battle under the banner of the cross.''

The people answered with shouts of ''Victory, victory in Jesus!''

Writing in 1909, Anderson and Watson, in their book, *Far North in India,* say of the convention's power, ''Each year since 1905, the Sialkot convention has been the occasion for fresh baptisms of the Spirit unto sanctification, unto prayer, unto praise and service. The influence has been felt in every part of the mission field. Recent conventions, far from losing their power, have gained in actual power, even where the manifestations were neither so unusual or so dramatic. Thus the Great Builder of the kingdom, having granted numerical successes, poured out His Spirit upon the rapidly growing Church, that its life might be purified and it might enjoy spiritual power in its expanded activities.''

Truly the second convention, 1905, was gloriously marked with spiritual manifestations which were to be felt throughout the nation, touching as it did ministers, American, English, Scottish, Canadian as well as native, of various denominations. These on returning to their fields of endeavor took back to their stations the power which they had received at Sialkot. Thus Spirit-endowed through Hyde's prayer work, they were to start afresh revival fires wherever they labored.

Mary Campbell gives us a glimpse into the workings of the convention among the girls of the school
she conducted in these words:

"One night a large group of girls rushed into the
room after the meeting in the big tent. They said
they had been in heaven and looking into their faces
one could not well deny it. They had heard a wonderful message on 'The Church as the Bride of
Christ,' and their hearts were full as they realized
the wonderful things God was waiting to do for His
people.

"The room was quickly filled, and people were
sitting on the verandah and out in the courtyard.
Hours passed like moments, and none was aware, so
spontaneous was the praise and so real the intercession. Only the day when accounts are settled will
reveal the victories of that night."

The effect upon the native Christians was tremendous, for it showed them the possibilities of
divine strength and achievement for the kingdom
which was within their grasp.

"A young Mohammedan girl," writes Emma
Anderson, "had become a Christian and in that
room was given to her such a burden for her unsaved
relatives as just broke the hearts of those who listened . . . A group of young Christian girls had come
many miles from another province and each girl
brought a hungry heart. They listened to a message
on the Holy Spirit, and more than anything else
they wanted His infilling. It was terrible to watch
the agony on their faces, but the longer they prayed
the greater became their distress . . .

"They accepted by faith. At once their sorrow
was turned to joy and their hearts filled with praise.

The light of heaven lit their faces. I cannot forget their eagerness to go back to Rajputana and tell how great things God had done for them."

It was in this convention that Hyde's obedience to God became absolute. He learned as an adopted son of India that he must not hurry the Holy Spirit. It was here he laid the foundation for the last seven years of his life, which, in fact, was his season of reaping. Until now he had been sowing; but after this convention he was to see the results of his spiritual planting.

So simple was his trust, so explicit his obedience, that once when the lunch bell rang, Hyde, in the prayer room, looked up into the face of God and whispered, "Father, is it Thy will that I go?" After a pause, the answer evidently came, and he responded, "Thank you, Father," arose with a smile and went to lunch.

And at the table where hungry souls were waiting, each one recognized that John had been in holy converse with his Lord. As he had fed on heavenly manna so he in turn refreshed their waiting hearts.

During this convention he received the promise that as Abraham of old he should have a spiritual progeny. At one time while he was in the prayer room he was told to arise and do a certain thing. He arose and made a confession that God wanted him to perform a task which he was to do unwillingly, saying, "Pray for me, brethren, that I may do this joyfully."

He went out and performed the distasteful task, returned with triumph written on his face, for in obeying, God had opened the future to him, and promised that many souls should be his.

"He entered the hall with great joy," writes
Francis McGaw, "and as he came before the people,
after having obeyed God, he spoke three words in
Urdu and three in English, repeating them three
times, '*Ai Asmani Bak,*' 'O Heavenly Father.' What
followed who can describe. It was as if a great ocean
came sweeping into that assembly, and 'suddenly
there came a sound from heaven as of a rushing
mighty wind, and it filled all the house where they
were sitting.' Hearts were bowed before the divine
presence as trees . . . before a mighty tempest."

When that breath of heaven came into the room
with John's return, hearts were melted, open confession broke forth, and numerous people sought
and found the Pearl of Great Price. It was this holy
presence which set Hyde apart from others, who had
not lingered in the prayer chambers so long and so
earnestly as he.

Referring to Hyde, a veteran missionary wrote,
"There were some who knew that God had chosen
and ordained them to be 'watchmen.' There were
some who had lived for long so near Jehovah that
they heard His voice and received orders directly
from Him about everything, even as to when they
were to watch and pray, and when they were to sleep.
Some watched all night long for nights, because God
told them to do so, and He kept sleep from them
that they might have the privilege and honor of
watching with Him over the affairs of His kingdom."

A final glimpse is granted us into that prayer
room which was Hyde's headquarters, where he met
the Spirit of God in direct communion. Missionaries.
who lived in the spiritually cold admosphere which

fringed heathenism could only marvel of the sense
of God's presence. Said one such, "At once you
knew you were in the holy presence of God, where
there could be only awful reality. Others in the room
were forgotten except when the combined prayers
and praises made you realize the strength and power
and sympathy of such fellowship. The hours of
waiting on God in communion with others were
precious times, when we waited on God to search us
and to speak to us — together interceding for others,
together praising Him for Himself and for His
wonder-working power . . .

"Some went to bed early, some prayed for hours,
some prayed all night, some went to the meetings
and some to the prayer room, some praised, some
sat to pray, some kneeled, some lay prostrate on
their faces before God just as the Spirit of God bade
them. There was no criticism in this holy atmosphere, no judging of what was being done or said.

"Each one realized that all superficialities were
put away, and that each was in the awful presence
of the Holy God."

This was the atmosphere that Hyde's prayer dili-
gence did much to create, and from this inspirational
assembly missionaries who had been filled with the
Holy Spirit went out into their Indian spheres to
work marvels for the kingdom, and to lay the foundation on which the present mass movement toward
the kingdom is now being built.

Among those men stood one, supremely paying
the price demanded for this glorious anointing, John
Hyde, and from these conventions he went forth not
only transformed in spiritual essence, but with a
new name, that of "Praying Hyde."

CHAPTER VI

FOLLOWING THE GLEAM

Praying Hyde upon returning home resumed his own village work where he left it before the convention of 1905. There was much for him to do, and with his heart aflame he threw himself boldly into days of visitation and nights of prayer. He knew no end to his strength as he daily tapped the reservoir of divine power.

Throughout the remainder of 1905 and until the 1906 convention he has left no specific record of his labors, save that with his little tent and his faithful native workers he kept diligently at the task of winning converts as God gave him grace.

During 1906 he began to have other visions of Christ. At the previous convention he had seen the Master suffering as a dog and finally dying for him, but now he was to look with the eye of faith and behold Jesus on the Throne, the glorified Christ as the Lamb of God. Praying Hyde entered into a mystical fellowship with God where the sufferings of the Lamb became a part of his own feeling element. Christ to him was the Head of his life and the Nerve Center which controlled his daily deeds.

When the 1906 convention arrived John was on hand among the first workers, and no sooner was the prayer room opened than he took his accustomed place of leadership. During this convention often while in the room of petition he would break out in weeping over the sins of the world and especially for Christ's sons and daughters.

With a shout he would quote, "Ye shall be sorrowful, but your sorrow shall turn into joy" (John 16: 20-22). Then his tears dried and his face shone with a glorious luster as joy swept through the room and hearts were soon in prayer.

"Thank God, He has heard our prayers," said a minister who was present at this convention, "and poured out the Spirit of grace and intercession upon so many of His children. For example, I saw a Punjabi brother convulsed and sobbing as if his heart would break. I went up to him and put my arms about him, and said, 'The blood of Jesus Christ cleanseth from all sin.' A smile lit up his face. 'Thank God, Sahib,' he cried, 'but oh, what an awful vision I have had! Thousands of souls in this land of India being carried away by the dark river of sin! They are in hell now. Oh, to snatch them from the fire before it is too late.'"

Similar visions seemed to mark many during this and other conventions. Some of the Indian girls, after making confession of their sins, would enter into a semi-trance, so customary among the Indian religious leaders, during which time they reported to have seen heaven, the angels, and Christ in the glory world. Some make a point of the fact that Indians are naturally meditative and as such are given to visions, nevertheless these praying Christians beheld inner glories often denied others.

Praying Hyde's burden during this convention was one of intercession, for to him the burdens of others had become a living reality, and his soul was weighted down with the sense of sin which ruled the land. He was brokenhearted for the sins of others, and in agony his soul cried out to God for their salvation. This is the true meaning of intercession and Hyde learned to drink thus of the Master's cup.

McGaw cites an example where an Indian girl at the convention had been forced by her father to give up her faith in Christ's saving power. In the prayer room she became burdened for her sins, and in confession poured out the bitter agony which had been dammed up in her consciousness. After confession she was struck with an inexorable conviction for her unbelief.

She fell on her face in prayer, and the burden which she had borne alone was quickly cast as a pall upon the souls of others, and they too entered into her grief. "One could almost see the springing tendrils of her heart as the power of the love of Christ came upon her. Then she asked us to pray for her father."

The Christians began to pray, "and suddenly the burden of that soul was cast upon us, and the room was filled with sobs and cries for one whom most of us had never seen or heard of before. Strong men lay on the ground groaning in agony for that soul. There was not a dry eye in the place until at last God gave us the assurance that prayer had been heard and out of Gethsemane we came into the Pentecostal joy of being able to praise Him that He had heard our cry."

Many who were in that all-night meeting of petition said they would never forget the memory of that blessed season of prayer and worship. "It was a time when God's power was felt as I never had felt it before," says one who was there.

Out of that service came souls with a transformed vision which gave a new meaning to obedience. They saw as Hyde had already learned that even in the smallest things God's sons must listen for His command and obey without questioning the divine will.

Returning to Ludhiana after the convention, Praying Hyde looked forward to his own village work. This year and especially the following spring he was to face a new difficulty which brought him no little concern. The plague with regularity swept over India during John's twenty years' residence. Writing under date of April 4, 1907, to Martha Gray, he says:

"The plague this year, especially in North India and the Punjab is very bad. Scarcely a place is free from it, and in many places many are dying. There are preventive measures, but the people are slow to use them, and accept things fatalistically often. My own belief grows that it is because of the sins of India which are very great, especially idolatry and the rejection of Christ who now for many decades has been presented to them."

During those plague times John lived true to his new name of Praying Hyde. When he met with the Christians who were suffering with the disease, many of whom he thought would die without divine aid, he went to the great Physician, believing that the "prayer of faith shall save the sick and the Lord shall raise him up."

"I have seen remarkable answers to prayer for the recovery of people from the plague," he says. "Jesus is living and can bring and remove pesti-

lence. Have we laid hold of Him and found deliver
ance from sin's plague?''

During the first part of April, 1907, he had just
returned from his village tours, and pressed for
time he wrote Miss Gray from the railroad station,
saying he was well. Thinking upon the rich harvest
of wheat, barley, and other grains which was just
ripening and ''is going to be tremendous,'' he is
constrained to lift his spiritual eyes and wonder
about the harvest of souls. ''I long night and day,
praying exceedingly for the harvest of souls in
India.''

When the hot weather came on in the summer of
1907 John with a group of like-minded believers,
including Pengwern Jones, went to Murree, a hill
station on the way to Cashmere. While this was set
apart as a period of physical escape from the heat's
devastating effects, it was supremely a time of
prayer and spiritual refreshing.

Says Jones, ''The Spirit moved them to arrange
for a week or ten days of waiting on the Lord while
there.''

When news scattered that the prayer sessions
were being conducted, others hearing of this came
and joined with the group. Several leaders of the
Sialkot convention were there with Praying Hyde.
Jones and Hyde were billeted together, and the
room, as Jones remarks, ''became a little heaven
and the memories of it will never be effaced.''

Being entertained by the McCheyne Patersons,
along with the other guests, Hyde found the fellowship was perfect. He was full of humor, and his
features marked with sadness became lighted with

joy as he shared the fellowship of these Christian brethren.

At the table the conversation led forth each one into the soul's green pastures as Hyde unburdened his heart and gave a glimpse of the glory he had experienced through prayer. Often his place was vacant, and well did the hostess know where he was. However beautiful the fellowship of the saints, Praying Hyde was anxious that nothing, not even this sacred privilege, should be permitted to come between him and Christ.

Jones gives us a picture of him, saying, "He was always on his knees clothed in a heavy overcoat when I went to bed, and on his knees long before I was up in the morning, though I was up with the dawn. He would also light the lamp several times in the night, and feast on some passage of the Word, and then have a little talk with the Master. He sometimes remained on his knees the whole day.

"At other times he would come with us to the services and spend the time in prayer in the vestry adjoining the church. The services were full of power, every word seemed to reach the heart of men. It was not the power of the messages, but the power of prayer that did it all. How easy it was to speak; there was an atmosphere of prayer."

Hyde stayed in the vestry throughout most of those meetings, to be joined by others as soon as the services were finished. His soul had envisioned the intercession of Christ and never again did he want it to lapse from memory. He kept it alive by being an interceder along with his Master, and even though he had come to the hills for physical recuperation, more glorious to him was the privilege of recharging the energies of his soul by prayer.

During this time of refreshment a soul-crushing burden for the Europeans at the station seized him. And for the next two or three days he did not go to bed, nor did he leave the room for his meals. Often he left untouched the food which was sent up to his room. When Jones came into the room, he would kneel beside his friend's bed that together they might share the burden.

On Saturday night Hyde was in the throes of soul agony as Paterson and Jones tried to assist him in his task of intercession. "It was a vision to me," says Jones, "of real agonizing intercession. He seemed to say like Jacob of old, 'I will not let Thee go,' and yet in the determination there was deep humility and loving pleading."

At two o'clock in the morning there came a knock at the bedroom door, and Paterson whispered to Jones that it must be his wife calling them to retire. Instead it was a letter addressed to Praying Hyde from a lady who was staying in the largest hotel in the place, requesting them to hold a service for the Europeans in the hotel drawing room.

Hyde read the letter, jumped up from his knees, and exclaimed, "That is the answer to my prayers. I *know* now that the Lord heard me."

As an immediate answer was requested, Praying Hyde urged his friends to make the response at once, even though the servant who had brought the message had already left for another place. Of course Paterson dispatched the promise that the service would be held.

Hyde's face shone with a divine glow when the request was answered, for he realized that God had again given him a burden of prayer and in response He Himself had sent an urgent answer in the middle of the night. And when meeting time came, John did not go with the group, remaining rather at his bedside on his knees that he might share his praying power with those who conducted the service.

That night when Hyde did attend service in the Scottish church such "heavenly joy lighted his features that it was contagious." Praying Hyde during those days of retreat loved the Book, and but few times was he far away from it. His Bible was always in his hand, and even over the morning cup of tea, he fed the souls of his friends with the Bread of heaven.

When he knelt to pray, the Bible was opened before him, and his hands rested on it, as though he gained strength therefrom to believe that he received the petition desired of the Lord. He lived thus face to face with Christ and daily rested on God's promises. He always had a spiritual morsel to give those who were with him, and by his own closeness to God he was able to lead others into the divine presence.

A Christian friend was in Murree at the same time, doing duty with the English troops, and fellowshiped with Praying Hyde. This soldier affirms that Hyde would remain for days so under the prayer burden that it seemed he must break. "But after whole nights of prayer and praise he would appear fresh and smiling in the morning," writes the soldier. "God was teaching us wonderful lessons during those times. He wanted us to endure hardness as a good soldier of Jesus Christ.''

The soldier felt that the source of Hyde's strength for such strenuous prayer vigils came from the admonition in II Timothy 1:8, where Paul says, ''Be thou partaker of the afflictions of the gospel *according to the power of God.*'' Hyde learned how to suffer and endure as upheld by the power of God. So in all his needs and tireless journeys it was God's strength upon which he drew. He told his friends that since he had learned this lesson he had very seldom, if ever, felt the least bit weary or tired, though at times there were weeks when he slept little more than a few hours.

Praying Hyde expressed the thought in the words, ''No man ever need break down in the ministry of intercession through overstrain.'' While in the hills he also taught his friends that another source of his daily strength was found in joying in the Lord. He could pray, intercede, go down to the lowest pit of burden bearing, all with grace and strength, for when he came out of it his face shone with a divine radiance, which he thought of as the smile of God reflected from his own countenance.

John's last message to the group before leaving for Ludhiana and the Sialkot convention was on Paul's wishing himself to be anathema for the sake of his kinsmen (Romans 9:1-3). Thinking upon this in light of his own experience Hyde said to his friends that such was the perfect expression of each of God's children when they learned to go down into the valley of sorrow so that others might be born into the kingdom. That message caused the group to break down in weeping and prayer, for God was leading John along gently until he was to be able to ask God for a certain number of souls each day — *and win them.*

Hyde lifts the veil on his activities after the Sialkot convention of 1907 when he writes to Miss Gray under date of November 14, saying, "Our mission annual meeting is just over. There is no change in my location. God is good to me. Our district work is blessed too, as there were fifty baptisms during the past year, mostly men. Two of our workers have been greatly blessed too.

"One looks for a break among the Hindus and Mohammedans, so great is the interest. It is so everywhere. And the revival has so stirred faith and given such visions from the blood and revealed such mighty workings of Christ in many lives that the hope is very definite of Jesus being about to open the eyes of the Hindus and Mohammedans. Pray much for us."

Up until now this was the best year Hyde had seen, from the standpoint of conversions. He refers here to the Sialkot revival which had really begun to break through in 1904, increasing in spiritual intensity among the Christians in 1905. Never before did he report so many conversions or baptisms as now. He is gradually seeing the effects of those long years of prayer. It is at the coming Sialkot convention in 1908 that his faith is really to be applied to asking for a definite number of conversions each year.

The foregleam of the breaking through of the revival came into evidence by the middle of February, 1908. He again writes to his Christian Endeavor supporters in Illinois. "I am in the dis-

trict," he says, "at a place called Moga, a town of
several thousand in a populous region. The work is
taking root here . . . " Here he is beginning to
practice his method of missionary work which was
revealed to him at an earlier Sialkot convention,
that is, staying at a place until some spiritual results
are seen.

"There is seldom a day without a baptism. For
some time now I have never come into the district
without baptisms. And it is getting so that one's
heart is not full of peace if a day passes without one
at least. Yesterday it was a boy. Today another
whom he brought. It seems to depend on our nearness to God. Ask prayer for me that He may continually hide me under the shadow of His hand.
Praise the Lord! He has given me the spirit of
praise."

John opened the treasury chest of his heart and
shows us its workings. He had come into such nearness and intimate contact with God that it bursts
through in his letters.

"Praise is the King's Highway," he continues,
"Would we enthrone Him on earth? Would we
make Him a highway on which to come and bless?
Ask and employ the spirit of praise, in prayer and
song and teaching and exhortation. God is working wonderfully in India and in all the earth these
two or three years. He is preparing to work so
much more wonderfully also. There is so much to
praise Him for, and there are great difficulties waiting to fall as we compass them with our praise of
Him who has come down among us."

That summer at Winona, Howard Agnew Johnson
in speaking of Hyde's work said, "In the north of

India he is known as the man who prays much and sleeps little." From a letter written by Rev. C. H. Bundy to the American church we learn that in September, Hyde held meetings at the Training School and the Boys' Boarding School. "The meetings developed real power from the first and all felt that we have been greatly blessed."

Hyde is spoken of as "the most deeply spiritual man in India" by those who knew him at this time.

During the first part of March, 1908, he made another tour of his villages and on returning to Ludhiana on March 25, he speaks of how good God has been to him during that time. He anticipates the future which is about to break with increased soul-winning power when he says, "How full we should be of thanksgiving . . . for what has come, and especially the thanksgiving of faith for what is to come."

During the previous ten days he had been in a Christian colony of the mission with Jalal Masih, a native preacher. He says, "They own their land and are farmers. There had been heavy quarrels among them and other sins also. Before the meeting, prayer had been going on for some weeks, and we were delayed in going a week which led to more prayer and real looking to God.

"How wonderful was the blessing. On the way Jalal was deeply convicted and handed me 10 rupees ($3.33) in payment of something wrong in his money dealings with me. In the meeting he was still convicted. With one or two exceptions all confessed their sins openly and by name and not a few with great humiliation.

"God blesses much the open confession of sins. It works great cleansing and fear in everyone's heart. The women were not yielding and the pastor's wife with her tongue and severity was the hindrance chiefly."

True to his prayer habit, when there was difficulty, John "could not lie down and sleep but knelt by my bed all night . . . the next day the women broke down and the pastor's wife was in the lead."

In a report of a meeting which he held at Almora, a hill station where Mr. A. McGaw was in charge, he says that God's Spirit mightily moved upon the people, "One practical result coming out of this meeting is their promise (of nearly all) to give the tenth to the Lord. The congregation including the girls and boys must be some 150 or 200. This shows how He is working all over India. The call is for watchmen, and I am a watchman. Isaiah 59:16; Isaiah 62:1, 6, 7."

When summer came and the hot weather made it imperative that Praying Hyde go to the mountains, his friend and companion McGaw persuaded John to spend the summer with his family in the hills. He was provided with a room which was separate from the main part of the house so that he might have seclusion for intercession with the Master. When he arrived it was evident that he was bowed down with soul travail. When mealtime came, more than likely John was absent, and his host on going to the room would find him lying in agony or walking up and down "as if an inward fire were burning in his bones."

Said Hyde, "This is the fire of which our Lord spoke when he said, 'I came to cast fire upon the earth,' and how would I that it were already kindled. But I have a baptism to be baptized with, and how I am straitened till it be accomplished."

His fasting was not freighted with hunger, for usually when his host asked him to eat, he would reply, "I am not hungry," though he had been for many meals without food, or even days. There was a greater hunger eating at his soul, which could be satisfied only by prayer. This spiritual hunger had swallowed up his physical appetite and desire.

One thought filled Hyde's mind during the summer — the thought that Christ still agonizes for souls. He felt that even today in the Lord's ministry of intercession this agony was as real as when He blessed the earth with His personal touch. Step by step he was entering into a soul agony which assumed ever increasing proportions.

McGaw says though he was always in prayer, and ate and slept little, still he was in no wise dull or poor company, but was bright and cheery. The little McGaw children enjoyed the presence of "Uncle John," as they called him, very much, for he often played with them and was always ready with a congenial smile.

"Yet even the little ones appeared to realize that this was no time for play. They were wonderfully subdued and quiet in his presence in those days, for there was a light on his face that told of communion with another world," affirms his host at the time.

People were attracted to him, and often came with their own soul needs, requesting that Praying Hyde take time to ask a blessing upon them. Though always in prayer or communion, still he had time to speak of spiritual things to any who approached him, or to enter into their trials with the patience of one who knew how to suffer.

During that summer, friends were deeply concerned lest his body break under the strain of his prayer life, but marvelously he was sustained by an unseen Power. Whether he agonized voicelessly or with great weeping for India's millions, his face was lighted with a glow of hope. He had discovered that his hope was in the love and power of God, who knew not how to disappoint a waiting saint.

Nor was all that summer spent in agony, for at times his soul would lift forth its praises as it was flooded with melody. Then he would sing, but as his host remarked, "They were always songs in the night." During the days he did not lose sight of the lost and dying millions in his own district, but at night God would come and his voice would break forth in melody.

Often he would cry. "Father, give me these souls, or I die." It had been his prayer for some time that he should burn out in prayer rather than rust out in indolence. And to those closest him, the wick of his life's candle seemed to flicker lower now than ever.

God however was not yet through with him, for he was now at the threshhold of his greatest soul-winning days. He had learned how to enter into the Holy Spirit, and to visualize in his own life the suffering of Christ. Now God was to send him forth praying definitely for a certain number of souls, and year by year he was to win that many or more. He had met God face to face in prayer and through this came spiritual anointing and soul-communion with the divine.

Praying Hyde had walked all the way up to God's throne of grace and lived now where he could face the Heavenly Father with definite requests and know that they would be forthcoming. The secret of this was his living constantly in an intercessory mood. Other men who knew him wondered whether or not this might be the norm for the Christian life of all believers. Some doubted that it could be achieved, but all were assured that this alone was the secret of Praying Hyde's power with God and his influence over the Indian Church.

Chapter VII

THE HARVEST OF HIS PRAYERS

For many years now Praying Hyde had been prevailing before God for the outpouring of the Holy Spirit in revival power. As a result the Sialkot revival had spread the holy fire of salvation to various sections of India. Prayer conferences had sprung up, and in special preaching missions there had been evidences of God's workings. Even in individual, or personal evangelism, where Hyde was always at his best, there had been unusual results.

It occurred to him during the year 1908, at about the time of the annual Sialkot convention, to become specific in his asking. He took the courageous step of asking God for one soul each day of that year. This required a boldness of faith where he dared not entertain even the smallest element of doubt.

His soul was flooded with the sweet assurance that this was not beyond God's power to achieve through his own life. Friends who saw him at the time recognized that the strained, agonizing look which he had borne left his face, and in its stead came a calmness of purpose and a tranquillity of repose he had never before known.

When he spoke it was with a new confidence born of boldness in attempting the unusual for God, and then began a new life work for this apostle of prayer.

He measured the meaning of such a prayer, knowing full well there would be many long nights of petition without sleep, tedious journeys, tenting in the villages until results were produced, visiting, tramping, working in the rain, chill by night and heat by day. But he dared pay that price. He had heard the Good Shepherd's voice saying, "Other sheep I have which are not of this fold." And it was his undying desire to bring those sheep into Christ's fields of glory.

Hyde had mastered the art of personal evangelism, and it was a familiar picture to see him at the convention or in a native village lay his hands on a man's shoulders, look him earnestly and keenly in the eyes, and then plead the cause of Christ with him until native and preacher were on their knees seeking salvation. Once the victory was won and the assurance of forgiveness received, Hyde would baptize the person wherever he might be, in the village, by the roadside, at the convention, or anywhere.

At the break of the 1908 convention, where the crowd was to number up to 2,000, Hyde was present, for he realized that Dr. Gordon, who had charge of all arrangements for eating, sleeping, housing the meetings, preparing the prayer rooms, etc., would need the assistance of his prayers. As Gordon and his helpers were putting up dozens of tents, arranging cooking facilities, and caring for the scores of necessary details, Hyde and a few others were already on their faces praying, praising and pleading that theirs might be a claimed blessing.

As soon as the large tent was up, Hyde and others entered to dedicate it to the Lord. By the first night of the convention the two prayer rooms were opened and Hyde was busy bombarding the skies for salva-

tion and honor and glory. Those who were present
at the meeting say there was little gossip of the ordinary nature, for there was a seriousness which gave
the congregations the expectancy of holy things and
crowded out the usual run of friendly activities and
interests.

In the dining tent where hundreds were eating
they lifted the Glory Song until Pengwern Jones
says he heard it sung as never before on land or sea,
"and I longed to go to glory then and there to begin
this glory life. Food was left and got cold before
we could eat it, but our hearts had been warmed
with the fire of His love burning within."

Jones affords us an intimate picture of Praying
Hyde in the prayer room, which was in the Scottish
church, where some of the seats had been moved
aside and a carpet covered the open space. Sometimes there were hundreds of people present, and at
others only half a dozen. On his face in the midst of
the people was this apostle of prayer. We listen
as he utters a petition and then waits, longs, again
repeats the words many times, until finally his whole
soul is aflame with belief and he feels the assurance
that his is the petition desired of the Lord.

One particular night he prayed that he might
"open his mouth wide that He might fill it" (Ps.
81:10). He repeated this scores of times, emphasiz-
ing "wide ... wide ... wide ... *Wide* ... *WIDE!*
... *WIDE!* ... "

When that prayer was finished many were weeping, for they had caught a glimpse of the inner soul
of the man, the man who learned to know the mind
of God and to pray in the will of his Heavenly
Father.

Or again we see him as he arises and puts his arm around the neck of a praying, seeking brother. With his open Bible handy, he reads an appropriate Scripture passage, and before long together saint and seeker stand and rejoice in the song, " 'Tis done, the great transaction's done."

Once in the convention when he wanted to be alone, he climbed the church belfry that he might have a shut-in closeness with his Lord. There in the dark of night he poured out his soul unto God, and though others heard the echo of his voice only God caught the true meaning of his spirit. It was thus he wrestled with God.

It seemed that during the entire time but few hours passed without his being in the prayer room. A sixteen-year-old boy had carried Hyde's bedding and carefully made the bed, but it was never used during the convention. Often he would go to a corner of the filled prayer room, throw himself prostrate on the floor, and there sleep, if it could be called sleep, as he rested his soul for another period of prevailing before God.

During the whole ten days it is doubtful whether he went to the dining room for his meals more than once or twice. Sometimes his boy or *Gulla*, the sweeper, or a friend, would take a plate of curry and rice to the room of prayer, and if convenient or he felt the need of it, he would move aside and partake of the food. Often his boy cried because Hyde would not eat and sleep as he should.

This became contagious and other missionaries and Indians followed in his spiritual steps. Once Hyde told a friend that he dreaded the thought of anyone's trying to follow his example.

Few times during the convention did he come to the platform to give an address, feeling that his place was in the prayer room, but when he spoke it was with tremendous power and spiritual quickening. He spoke in Urdu, which he used aptly and well, speaking in a quiet voice that rang with a divine challenge. When friends would caution him, "You will kill yourself if you continue working as you are," after some such message which followed a strenuous season of prayer, he would say, "Give your life for God and men." And this was his one concern. He counted not his life dear unto himself if he could but win souls.

At one convention, either this or a later, his message was on the cross. Coming from the prayer room his life was bathed in a heavenly glory which had surcharged both voice and being. Carefully and graphically he outlined the meaning of the cross, its suffering and sorrow. Step by step he led the audience to see the cross and its baseness as Christ hung thereon for our sins.

Then he cried, "It is finished!" The effect was electric, for to Hyde that cry was a shout of victory. He pointed out how we are to shout in the face of seeming failure and discouragement, the shout of victory. "We too," said the speaker, "may stand by the cross and shout, 'Victory, victory, victory!' And this shout is the real victory when we can be triumphant in face of darkness."

Said M. Waldegrave, son of Lord Radstock, "I generally go to my tent after every service and write the message that I have heard to my wife, but Mr. Hyde's message just delivered seems so sacred and appealing that I dare not try to write it."

When asked further about the cross, he said, "For a year now I have been fascinated by the cross. I cannot speak on any other subject now." He had lived the cross experience by praying himself into the attitude of suffering and agony, and it was natural for him to give voice to the true meaning of Christ's cross-ministry.

Leaving the convention he resumed his village ministry, traveling, pleading and praying with hungry souls. Few details remain of the year's work, except that he, along with native workers, covered his field diligently and well. Wherever he found souls, the message of the cross was told them with kindness and a spirit aflame with zeal for Christ.

When the time approached for the 1909 convention, he checked the number of converts who had been won to the Lord and they totaled four hundred, or more than the one a day, for which he had asked the Lord at the previous convention. He made little of this achievement, for he recognized that it was only through the Lord that this victory was possible.

He accomplished this soul-work by devoting his nights largely to prayer and his days to a hand-to-hand grip with souls. He was not content merely to sow Gospel seed in a heart. He wanted to remain with that person, water the spiritual seed with heavenly dew, and be present when the harvest of salvation was reaped. When at all possible, he climaxed each decision for the Master with baptism.

At the 1909 convention God laid it upon him to ask for two souls each day of the coming year. The glory of this convention and Hyde's prayer life

marked a higher tide than previously. The burden
of his message was, "Ask, and it shall be given you;
seek, and ye shall find; knock, and it shall be opened
unto you." This he looked upon as a prayer life of
intensified desire, rising from climax to climax until
the very gates of heaven had been petition-stormed
and faith-bombarded.

"When we keep near to Jesus," he said, "it is
He who draws souls to Himself through us, but He
must be lifted up in our lives; that is, we must be
crucified with Him."

This was the keynote of Hyde's power as a soul-
winner. He had been crucified with Christ, self had
been destroyed that the glory of the Master might
shine through his actions. "If not 'buried' the
stench of the old man will frighten souls away. If
these three steps downward — *crucified, dead and
buried with Christ* — are taken as to the old man,
then the new man will be revived, raised and seated
— three corresponding steps upward which God
permits us to take."

It was this experience, he felt, which was to qual-
ify soul-winners for the task of taking men alive for
the Master.

Back to the field and to hungry hearts he went
with his prayer for two souls each day ringing to
high heaven, and when the 1910 convention opened
he had seen eight hundred souls accept the Master
as their Lord and Redeemer. In this he saw no
cause for glorying; rather he distinctly felt the
need for a greater humility, that self might be
plunged out of sight and Christ viewed by all.

Arriving at the convention, he once more took
hold of God for greater victories than before had

graced his labors. Deeper into the shadow of the garden of sorrow he went until he felt that God had laid on him the necessity of bearing the sin burdens of others. He began confessing their sins for them, and desired, were it only possible, to lay his life down that they might walk the Christ-way. This meant a daily dying for others, which he was gradually doing.

Little is recorded as to the work of that 1910 convention, though it was to be his last, except that God gave him the assurance that his trophies for the year were to be four souls each day.

For five years he had borne the prayer burden for the convention and each year it had weighed heavier and heavier on his heart. Before the convention he had spent many long nights in prayer until the burden had eaten into the fibre of his inner being. Those who saw him recognized that excruciating pain born of petition was written, chiseled on every feature of face and body.

"Yet his figure was almost transformed," says a friend writing in India, "as he gave forth God's own words to His people with such fire and force that many hardly recognized the changed man with the glory of God lighting up every feature . . . "

And when Hyde returned to the field, he lost sight of all else save those four souls each day. He once told a friend that if on any day four souls were not brought into the fold, at night there would be such a weight on his heart that it was positively painful, and he could not eat or sleep. Looking into his own heart, he sought for the obstacle, and of all things, he found it to be the lack of praise as often as any other hindrance.

His procedure in making up the lacking number
of souls for the lost days of ineffectiveness was
merely to begin to praise God beforehand for the
glory He was going to reveal and the souls He was
to draw unto Himself. This invariably, Hyde tes-
tified, enabled him to achieve the total number of
souls for a specific day or week.

Praying Hyde was now forty-seven years old.
Since he was forty he had been a shining light of
prayer, from which had winged forth the Sialkot
revival which revivified missionary work in North
India during those days, and was the means for the
quickening of many hundreds of souls. John was
within two years of heaven. His soul was seriously
engaged in this one endeavor, that of winning decisions for his Master.

He had little or no time for anything else but the
winning of souls. He was called throughout the
nation for revivals and spiritual life conventions,
and wherever the call came, if he had time, he always responded. Once while he was gone to Calcutta for a convention, time arrived for the annual
mission meeting, but Hyde was not there.

The mission officers, expecting everybody to be
present, discussed wiring Hyde to hasten on to the
assembly. A tide of bickering went back and forth
about such negligence, some saying, "I too would
have time for prayer if I neglected my other duties
as he does." Then Dr. Fife, a missionary with
whom he had been living, arose and took up the
absent brother's cause, saying, "Brethren, as I have
watched John Hyde this summer, and seen him hour
after hour, pale, weary, at prayer, I have come to
know that he has not chosen the easy part; and it is

my feeling if he is led of God to remain in Calcutta for the work there, he is doing it not to escape work, but for God's glory. I believe we should leave it to him to decide what his duty is."

This feeling prevailed and Hyde's case was dropped. But where during this time was the missing parson? He should have been there, for he had charge of two districts at the time, and there were reports and other necessary business demanding his attention. Here is what he was doing: attending to the business of his King.

Getting on the train at Calcutta in time to make the annual meeting, he traveled with a man in need of spiritual help, which at once he gave him. But by the time the train had reached the village where the seeker was to get off, he had not yet prayed through to victory. So Hyde, rather than lose a soul, decided to miss the assembly, and he too left the train.

When the man was converted, the train had already pulled out of the station. Hyde took the next train for Ludhiana where the assembly was meeting. Again the process was repeated, for Hyde had discovered another hungry soul. Leaving the train with the seeker, he once more missed his connection. This happened four times on that trip, but Hyde won four souls to the Master. The fourth man took John past Ludhiana, and so Hyde went on, winning the man in the end. On returning to the convention city, he discovered the meeting was over.

At another time Miss Wherry tells how she accompanied Hyde, along with Bible women and native preachers, on a village tour one day. The men went to converse with men, while the woman mis-

sionary and the Bible women went to the homes
where they brought spiritual help to the women.
The lady workers discovered a native woman who
had been looking for the missionaries and wanted
to be baptized.

"We called Mr. Hyde to examine her," says Miss
Wherry, "and before we left that village there were
ten souls added to the Christian community. Mr.
Hyde said, 'I was expecting ten, for this morning
in my prayer the figure ten was given me!' "

It was this that opened India to Hyde's entry.
He learned first to talk to God about souls and then
he kept after God's prospect until the daggers of
the Spirit had pierced through the life, and a new
name was written in heaven.

Another morning as Praying Hyde was reading
the Bible the number ten appeared in the passages
under consideration, which he took, after prayer,
as the number of souls to be given him that day. He
and his native workers started out on a journey of
some distance to a Punjab village. Their trail was
a road that banked a river, on which night travel
was extremely hazardous. During the morning he
met no one, nor did anyone offer him water or food,
but at length on reaching a village, his native helpers grew impatient and thought they had better
begin the return journey. But Hyde was not to be
budged, for his mind rang with *ten, ten, ten souls*.

Finally at a common cottage he asked for water,
and on being given a drink, he talked with the house-
holder who knew of Christ's work and power. Hyde
pushed home the thought that since the house had
entertained them in Jesus' name, why not let the
Master come in and abide with them.

On through the afternoon Hyde presented Christ, and pleaded with the family to be converted. Finally the native workers became indignant at the missionary's insistence, feeling they should long ago have been on their homeward way. But this man of God knew in his soul that here were converts to be won; so diligently he pressed Christ's claims and before long each member of the family was converted and together they were baptized.

Yet there remained *one of the ten* to be reached before the day's promise had been fulfilled.

When the evangelists urged Hyde to begin the homeward trip, the missionary, agony written on his face, asked, "What about that one?" Waiting for that tenth soul, even though the cart was in the road ready to proceed without him, he would not be moved. Later the evangelists confessed to McCheyne Paterson how domineering they had become toward the sulking preacher, but they could not forget the soul-cry, "What about that one?"

Soon the man of the cottage asked concerning the delay, seeing the evangelists were so anxious to be on their way, and Hyde told him about his promise of ten.

"Why, there he is," said the father, "my nephew whom I have adopted. He has been living with the rest of us, but has been out playing."

The lad, a bright intelligent boy, was brought in, told of the Master, and soon he too followed his family into the Christian fold.

"That is the ten," weary Hyde finally said, a gleam creeping from his eyes to light his entire countenance. And with good-bys spoken he was on his way home, light of heart and joyous of step.

Nor was there danger on that dark night trip along the lonely river, for Christ had walked before, preparing the way.

How then could such a diligent soul-hunter fail God in finding his four souls a day? The four and more were won day by day and occasionally God gave him an over-plus that Hyde's heart might be made to glory in the God of his salvation.

The secret of this victory is to be found in the long foundational steps he had taken in preparing his own soul for spiritual perseverance. He had been under the Spirit's personal tutelage for years, and now, face to face with God, he knew how to bring men face to face with the Saviour. His burdened soul, weighted with India's sins, created the right atmosphere in which to germinate Christian decisions when he taught the natives the glory of walking with Jesus along India's dusty roads of the commonplace.

Chapter VIII

ALONG THE INDIAN ROAD

Praying Hyde's India trek was climaxed by one motivating passion . . . he must fish for souls. Seeming to recognize the shortness of his own time, he was most careful and diligent in his approach to the wary soul-lost Indians. He loved his Master supremely, and the shower of this love fell upon the benighted people of India, whom he wanted to bring into the kingdom ere his fishing days were over. Several incidents have been recorded for us as to his spiritual beneficence toward those he would win.

There was a young Brahmin attending the Presbyterian mission school, whom Hyde had won completely and fully to personal fellowship with Jesus. Leaving school, he faced bitter opposition from his widowed mother and relatives, until he gave up his Christian confidence. His mother surrounded him with youths who were drunkards, and soon with joy she saw her son fall a victim to the drink demon. She knew her problem of keeping him from a return to Christianity had been thus solved.

Hyde, loving the lad as a brother, took him under his care, and finally won him once more to Christ. But the boy's struggle with drink was not over. He fought it with all his Christian powers, but in weak moments rum gained the upper hand. With no money to purchase drink, he would steal Hyde's clothes, sell them, and then go on a drunken orgy for days.

With a smile on his face, Praying Hyde, knowing the full redemptive power of Christ in his own life, would search for the lad, bring him home again, and tenderly nurse him back to Gospel hope. On one such spree, when Hyde's warm clothes had been sold, he met McCheyne Paterson, with whom he often spent the summer in the hills, and said, "I may not get up to you to the hills this summer; the Father evidently wants me to spend my hot weather in the plains, for 'I have no warm clothes left!'"

Gladly Hyde took the spoiling of his goods, that he might win the soul back to the ways of Christian joy and fellowship. At length the work was completely wrought and the boy became a fine Christian. During that last struggle the lad ran away from Hyde and went to Lahore, but on hearing that Hyde was at a certain place, he came back miserable and repentant.

Going to his room, the boy found the missionary praying. Opening his eyes, Hyde said, "I have just been praying that God would send you back to me, and see, He has answered."

It was often the custom of this man of prayer, on finding an Indian in need, to take his own clothes and give to them. Many times at the Sialkot convention, according to Mary Campbell who knew Hyde well, when the praying man would find a native with no blanket, he would go to his own bed, take off the blanket, and hand it to the native. And once when his own blanket had been given to one in need, he went to Paterson's bed, took his blanket and gave it also to another friend of the India road.

It was not at all uncommon for Hyde to take the coat off his back and give it to a needy native. This became so common that friends had to watch after his clothes, lest he be found in dire need.

But it was this self-sacrifice which won for him a way into the Indian heart. How could one turn down such a man's Saviour, a Saviour who had produced such a noble character as John Hyde?

Again, a Christian woman, who was a ticket collector, noticed John Hyde on a train going to Lahore speaking to a native lad, who was saying, "I am tired of this sort of thing — I am going to my companions, and have a good time."

Leaning over his seat, Hyde begged with tears in his eyes, asking, "Why will you leave the Saviour?" Finally the boy went on, forsaking Hyde and the love he showed. Said the Christian onlooker, "He knew the value of an immortal soul."

The next day the woman noticed the same boy return from Lahore, where he had been, and she said, "You have come back very soon." "Yes," he returned, "I am going back to him. I have not been able to sleep all night. I could not forget his tears."

Once when Hyde had lost a soul who had forsaken the Christian cause, the missionary never failed to pray that he would at length return. For some weeks this went on, until one day, while Hyde was conducting a meeting in a distant village, the person, tired and worn, walked in, his feet swollen.

When Hyde saw him, he knew the prayer for the man's salvation had been answered. Taking the man in his arms in Punjabi style, he made him lie down, and with his own hands rubbed those swollen feet until they were well once again. Years later when a friend spoke to the native about Hyde, he said, "I often see him in my dreams before me as of old."

Nor could India soon forget the man who had thus imprinted his character on the inner visions of her sons. Through love he wooed and won his converts to the Christ who taught the world that "God is love."

At another time, while Hyde was eating dinner, natives ran to him saying, "The pastor is ill, and his house is on fire." Rushing to the scene, he found the Indian pastor in the throes of great pain. Putting out the fire, Hyde came back to the preacher and prayed with him. On discovering that the sickness had its origin in conscience, he said, "I think it is God's will that you confess your sin in church before your congregation."

The native was carried to the church on his sickbed, from which he made an open confession of a deeply dyed sin, asking for forgiveness. At once the pain in both heart and body left him. Twenty members of the congregation made open confession of sins, and together they all wept their way through to a solid soul-foundation. The meeting lasted an hour and a half, after which Hyde and the others returned to finish their half-eaten dinner.

Another evening Hyde and his native helper were going to the hills for an evangelistic meeting. They had come third class to the foot of the hill, and had only enough money for a pony and a coolie between them. So by turns they rode the horse. When the Indian was riding, suddenly a huge tiger leaped over the pony and landed in the road just behind him, having missed his objective.

The frightened horse crashed into a run and sped on to the village, where on arriving the native preacher told the men about the incident, and a group returned to hunt for what might be left of Praying Hyde. They found him struggling up the road, having passed the very place where the tiger had been, but seeing nothing at all of the ravaging beast which must have slunk away in the jungles.

At the village a noble Christian work was achieved, with many souls being baptized. When they returned to their own place of abode, each rode a pony through the generosity of the Christian friends that were left behind. Said the native assistant, "We went there like beggars, but we returned like kings."

During another deputation trip, he and his workers had come to a village, and, on arising the next morning, Praying Hyde found his head driven through with pains which made even prayer excruciating. Since it was his custom to thank God in and for everything, he lifted his voice in praise to the Almighty for this experience. But he could not see how it would be possible to carry on with the outlined program.

Rethinking the situation, he decided that for his Master's sake such a little matter as a bed-confining illness should not deter him from his search for souls. So he ordered his helpers to carry his bed to a shady place where he would speak to the natives as occasion was granted.

Many of the village men were baptized Christians, though their wives had not yet made the decision for Christ, but as the women saw the Padri Sahib lying on his pallet, they came one by one to express

sympathy with him. This enabled him to bare his
heart to them, and to present personally Christ's
claim upon their souls. The words won lodgment,
and many of them were converted. Among themselves they discussed their baptism, and together
decided they should take the step as their husbands
before them had done. Having baptized a number
of those who had been converted, Praying Hyde
said, "I now see the reason for the severe head-
ache this morning. Without it I would not have
been enabled to win those women."

Hyde was naturally a morose fellow when left to
his own inclinations, but when thrilled by the electric
touch of the Spirit he was usually bursting with
heavenly joy. It was this characteristic of praise
in spite of circumstances which frowned upon the
day, that caught the attention of non-Christians.

One day, however, when he came to a village with
two of his native evangelists, he found little cause
for rejoicing. As they approached the town, they
had been discussing the reason why so few converts had been made in the place, and naturally
entered the city with heavy hearts.

But in the cart were the evangelists' children, who
had been won through Hyde's interest in them. The
little folk were not touched with the preachers'
lead-heartedness, and so they sang hymns and
Psalms, rejoicing in the joy of the Lord. Throughout the journey they had kept up a merry clatter
of singing and melody making. The spirit soon became contagious, and Hyde, with the others, shed
his gloom in a spell of song. So, singing and praising the Lord, they entered the center of the village.

When the villagers, who until then had closed tightly their hearts to the Lord's entrance, saw the joy and looked upon the now-happy faces of the Christian workers, they took an immediate interest in Hyde's message. One by one believers appeared in the group, until before the day was through a dozen showed living faith in Christ, and the preacher dared not refuse them Christian baptism.

Mr. Hyde often related an experience of a similar nature which occurred at a village of farmers where the Gospel had been preached for thirty years with no visible results. Coming to the town, the farmers said, as always, "Not now during the harvest, but later we will hear you." So early the next morning in a downcast spirit the workers decided to leave the stiff-necked people and let Jeremiah's words be true of them, "The harvest is past, the summer ended, and we are not saved."

Later in the day one of the workers suggested they all go to the village and sing the Gospel to the people, which accordingly was done. The entire group mustered their best singing voices, and put a not-felt melody into action. Throwing back their heads, they sang and *sang* the sweetest Gospel songs they knew. After midnight they retired to their tents, well determined in the morning to be off to another village where it might not be necessary to shake the unbelieving dust from their feet as they did in this town.

Next morning, as they were juggling together their personal effects in closing their unrewarded stay at this village, a young man rushed to them, begging them to remain yet awhile. He said, "The *Panchayat* (council) is in session now. No one is working this morning for they are considering whether or not to accept Christ and confess Him before all men.''

This was glad news and the Christian workers remained yet awhile for the town's decision. Shortly the young man came running back to them with the story that the council had decided to serve Christ. When Hyde approached them, he found fifteen men, mostly heads of families, who were prepared for Christian baptism. With glory breaking into song in his heart he performed the rite as already Christ had baptized them in their lives.

"This is the result of your singing last night," said the message bearer. "Remember last night how you sang:

'Lift up your heads, O ye gates,
And let the King of Glory enter in!'

And has He not entered in this morning?'' The message bringer himself had been converted and entered into the spirit of the meeting with a holy beauty shining from his sun-baked face.

Hyde often said that when he was slack in singing and in rejoicing audibly before the people he noticed that his converts were few. To alter the situation he began to sing joyously and openly in his meetings, and to lift a pean of praise before the people. This turn in affairs usually produced the desired effects and souls were won.

Deep-hearted in his success was his compassionate love for the Indian. There were no limits he would not go that he might win a soul. On the trains, riding as he often did, it made little difference whether he got off at his own destination, provided that by going farther he might win the person with whose soul he was at spiritual grips. Often he overrode his own ticket that he might master some life for Christ's cause.

One cold night while Praying Hyde was staying with a native evangelist, he tapped on the man's door. Because of the lateness of the hour, the man asked what Hyde wanted.

"Can you lend me a sheet for the night?"

"Where," in amazement asked the native, "are your own blankets?" And without waiting for the answer, he continued, "That drunken sot who was with you has gone off with them. He will sell them for drink and make a beast of himself. Do you know what a difficulty you make for us by such actions?"

Later, while telling the story to McCheyne Paterson, the evangelist owned with remorse his sorrow at the answer, for Hyde had gently said, calling him by name, "If the prodigal had come back to you, you would have taken a stick to him!"

Once Paterson and Hyde had gone to a church for a series of mission services, but as usual Hyde remained in his room for prayer and left the preaching to his friend. When he did appear, all noticed that his face was drawn in agony. "Night after night in the meeting," says Paterson, "the atmosphere remained cold and dead. Poor John seemed to shrivel up more and more. The burden on him was immense."

At the last service, John as usual was in his prayer room, and the meeting was tense and cold, until one of the natives came forward and asked to speak.

"I have had a controversy with God during this meeting and have not been out a great deal," he said. "You all know that a famous Persian carpet is for sale at this station. I made up my mind to buy it. If the price went high I was going to buy it for my office, and the government would pay for it [he was an official]; but if it went low, I would purchase it for my own room. Every time I came to these meetings that carpet started up before my eyes and kept me from getting a blessing. Now I have resolved that if that carpet sells dear I'll have it for myself, and if it sells cheap it will go in my office."

That broke the tenseness of the atmosphere and before the meeting, which John prayed into existence, had finished many more confessions were made. "What followed no pen can describe . . . On both sides of the divided church old enemies became friends and the Lord's glory melted the congregation together. It was a marvelous meeting, but Hyde had remained secreted with his Lord in prayer, where in fact the stumbling Persian carpet which stared the official in the face had been lifted up time and again."

Hyde's close walk with God had aroused spiritual difficulty in the community where an Indian doctor decided to test the preacher's daily life. Many had been converted and the native physician wanted to know whether or not Hyde's religion at home was as genuine as he claimed.

So he dispatched a friend to the missionary, affirming that he too was a Christian believer. Hyde at once opened his home to the Indian, and asked him to remain for several days. This fitted perfectly into the doctor's scheme, and so the native accepted the invitation. Living with Hyde, he had occasion to study the man in action.

After three or four days the man ran away and went to the doctor who sent him, saying, "He has no fault, that man has no fault; he is a god, he is a god, and not man!"

This was the answer which Hyde's personal life boomeranged to the doctor, and it was this life beyond a seeming fault which indelibly carved his features upon the Indians who came to know him. Is there little wonder then that a missionary remarked that had his bones consecrated India's soil, the non-Christians would have made his grave a shrine?

CHAPTER IX

EDGING TOWARD THE HEAVENLY KINGDOM

Hyde was now gradually edging toward the heavenly land, and was soon to finish his India trek upon which he had launched eighteen years earlier. At the close of the 1910 Sialkot convention he had been called to Calcutta for a revival. The friend with whom he stayed during this meeting noticed that each day the preacher had a fever.

Though weak in body, Hyde saw no occasion for being less diligent in his prayer ministry and preaching than before. He slept across the hall from his friend, and each night as he flashed on his light for his prayer at twelve, two, four and then at five, the friend would notice it.

For two weeks during the meeting this went on constantly, though during the day the fever began to rage higher and higher, until at length he was induced to visit a doctor.

"The heart is in a serious condition," said the physician after examination of the patient. "This is the most serious case I have ever run across. Your heart has been shifted out of its natural position on the left side to a place on the right. Through stress and strain it is in such a bad condition that it will require months of strictly quiet life to bring it back again to anything like its normal size."

That to John was a head-bending blow, for his schedule called for an active ministry of evangelism. He listened as the doctor continued:

"What have you been doing with yourself? Unless you change your whole life and give up strain, you will have to pay the supreme penalty within six months."

Here it was — the death knell sounding irrevocably in his ears with the crash of eternity in its boom.

There was but one thing to do: give up his ministry of intense intercession and live, or intercede and die. The words crept as a comfort through the desolate regions of his mind, "They loved not their lives unto the death." Was he willing to pay that price? He had always been willing, and at the end there was to be no shrinking. His plea had been, "Give me India, or I die!" And now with death's shoulder leaning up against the corner of his India tent, he was to go on to the end.

The Calcutta revival and the doctor's examination occasioned Hyde's absence from the annual mission meeting at which he was to give his report. Having written a six-page report, he wanted to mail it so that the conference would have it in time for their consideration. But he was seized with a severe head pain, brought on by the nightly fevers, and the year's review was never sent.

Though he knew his absence again would be misunderstood, Praying Hyde, now facing heaven's soon-to-open door, looked upon this as another weight added to his Christian cross, and was willing to be misrepresented and slandered for the Master's sake, who had died for him.

Said his Calcutta friend at the time, "Have we ever heard of a martyr who was so given up to the ministry of prayer that the strain of a daily burden brought him to a premature grave?"

Another Indian leader responded, "Not a premature grave; it was the grave of Jesus Christ. John Hyde laid down his life calmly and deliberately for the Church of God in India."

But in this weakened condition, Hyde's life was still on the search for souls, and his influence was being swept across the broad ocean of Indian life. A lady missionary began to read about his life of trust and prayer and in the end was so aroused to her own lack of prayer-burden that she gave herself day and night to intercession.

The anointing of God came upon her otherwise drought-stricken and lifeless service. She said, "I felt that at any cost I must know Him and this prayer life and so at last the battle of my heart was ended and I had the victory." In less than a year, she told a friend, her life had been transformed from a desert to a spiritual garden, and she reported more than a hundred conversions during the year.

"The spirit of earnest inquiry," she said two years later, "is increasing in the villages and there is every promise of a greater movement in the future than we have ever had. Our Christians now number six hundred in contrast to one sixth of that two years ago . . . "

Herrick Johnson, a McCormick classmate, was touched by Hyde's influence and entered into a life of spiritual conquest. He says, "Hyde was like a father. When duty called, the call was imperative.

He answered it . . . with unalterableness of purpose and that meant this or death. It seems God meant this and death . . . ''

In spite of this John's life went marching triumphantly on, shattering the placid ocean of India's religious life with the crashing thuds of his prayer, until those churning waves shall resound on the eternal shores.

On March 11, 1911, Praying Hyde's India labors were over and as a dying man he sailed for home by way of England. He had been in India about nineteen years — years packed to the full with thrilling soul conquests, and now when the cup of his services were brimming over, he was sailing home to die.

In the previous October his friend and beloved associate in the Gospel harness had gone on a furlough to Wales, and before leaving had invited Praying Hyde, when he should return to the homeland for his second rest in 1911, to visit him.

While on the steamer John had mislaid Pengwern Jones' Wales address and thought for a while that he would be unable to keep his promise. There was however another English missionary aboard from whom John was able to secure Jones' address. On arriving in England, he at once set off for Llangollen, where his missionary friend lived. Jones was at the time out visiting some acquaintances and when he returned home his wife said, "Guess who has come. Of all your numerous friends, which one would you like to see and have his company on this Good Friday?"

"Then she said, 'Go to the bedroom and see who is there having a wash.' I rushed upstairs and that

was the beginning of a month or two of a little
heaven on earth for me . . . What a privilege it
was to have one of the children of God who lives
in His very presence with us at the table. It became
the Lord's banqueting house, and we freely drank
of His Spirit."

Hyde expressed the wish to remain until Keswick
week, so he might attend the famous meetings with
two of his India friends, Jones and Paterson. Knowing that Hyde was to be present at the meetings,
the committee arranged for a prayer room as had
been the custom at Sialkot. But both Hyde and Paterson fell ill at the time and the plans did not
materialize. Hyde always felt that he wanted to
begin a prayer room at Keswick similar to the one
at Sialkot.

While in Wales he had the privilege of visiting
J. Wilbur Chapman, who was conducting a preaching mission at Shrewsbury. He and Jones decided
to attend the services, for Hyde had heard of the
evangelist's work. On arriving at the scene of the
meetings they found little evidence of interest. At
once it was suggested by their host that several
ministers gather with Jones and Hyde for the purpose of praying through for the mission.

"The ministers present, and they were a good
number," writes a spectator, "seemed to treat the
whole matter as a side show." Hyde found Chapman's message to be intense, but the results meager.

"I cannot leave a brother minister to bear this
burden alone," said Hyde, and invited his friend
Jones to join with him in a prayer siege. Hyde was
absent over Sunday to fill a speaking appointment
of his own, and on Monday when he returned to the

scene of the revival, he found a Mr. Davis, of the Pocket Testament League, ready to assist in the intercession. During this season of prayer the Spirit changed the atmosphere of Chapman's meetings, as is evidenced by a letter from the evangelist.

"At one of our missions in England," writes Dr. Chapman, "the audience was extremely small. Results seemed impossible, but I received a letter . . . saying that an American missionary known as 'Praying Hyde' would be in the place to pray God's blessings down upon our work. Almost instantly the tide turned. The hall was packed and my first invitation meant fifty men for Jesus Christ. As we were leaving, I said, 'Mr. Hyde, I want you to pray for me.'

"He came to my room, turned the key in the door, dropped on his knees, waited five minutes without a single syllable coming from his lips. I could hear my own heart thumping and his beating. I felt the hot tears running down my face. I knew I was with God.

"Then with upturned face, down which tears streamed, he said, 'Oh, God!' Then for five minutes at least he was still again, and when he knew that he was talking to God, his arm went around my shoulder, and there came up from the depths of his heart such petitions for men as I have never heard before, and I arose from my knees to know what real prayer was. We have gone round the world and back again, believing that prayer is mighty, and we believe it as never before."

For a week Hyde remained in the city, bearing the intercessor's burden for Chapman's work, and the influence of his prayers was to follow the evangelist around the world. When he returned to his friend's home in Wales, his face was drawn in agony and he was so weak he could scarcely speak.

"The burden was very heavy," he greeted his friend, "but my dear Saviour's burden for me took Him down to the grave."

Twice during this England visit, when he would have drawn people into the closer fellowship of prayer, some present at the meetings hindered, and one wonders what the results might have been had Hyde been privileged to establish the prayer rooms in Britain as he had done in India.

In North Wales he had been invited by the Presbytery to speak in various churches, where evident results followed his messages, though they were delivered in great physical pain. By popular demand he had been asked to address the Presbytery. At a great effort to himself he attended, to find a large audience awaiting him.

But something happened at the session, in spite of various notes being sent to the secretary, who denied the pulpit to Praying Hyde. Suffering then from severe headaches which in the end were to take his life, he endured the evident slight courageously as for the Master.

"They do not understand," Hyde simply said, "I know they do not want to be unkind. This is my cross which He wants me to take up and carry for Him."

It was this note of love and his ability to forget and forgive those who would injure him which made it possible for him so thoroughly to enter into the Master's fellowship.

Three characteristics marked Hyde's work wherever he labored. His was an ardent and passionate love for Christ. On one occasion he remarked, "Years ago I felt that I wanted to give something to Jesus Christ who loved me so, and I gave myself to Him absolutely, and promised Him that no one should come into my life and share my affection for Him. I told the Lord I would not marry, but be His altogether." It was the compassion of this love which enabled him to enter into a life of intercession.

Again, he passionately loved the people with whom he labored. No sacrifice was too great for him to make that the Indians might be reached. Entire nights of prayer, weeks of toil in the hot sun, days spent in evangelizing the villages when he should have been in the hills resting, were the signs of that love which in the end caused him to lay down his life for India.

Nor did he feel less regard for his fellow missionaries. He was careful to enter into their lives and help them with their burdens, and many were the nights he had spent praying for them. Often he recognized their difficulties, and with his hand laid gently on their shoulders, he would call them aside for a spiritual retreat where together they might unburden themselves at the Master's feet.

John Hyde's religion was not on dress parade, for he lived simply, yes, grandly, according to the pattern of Christ which he found written largely over the pages of the New Testament. When he left India his influence did not depart, for behind him were those streams of spiritual life which had founted in his prayers. Coming to the end, he faced it with courage, and his last thought was for those who would follow to walk his path on the Indian road.

Chapter X

SHOUTING THE VICTORY

Home-going to Hyde was not a difficult thought for he had lived so grandly the heavenly life and lisped so sweetly the heavenly song, that when he could lift his eyes and see through heaven's open gates, he looked upon death as a friend who was to conduct him into the King's presence.

He knew he was sick, and even though he could lengthen life by ceasing his intercession, still there was never a moment until the end that he was not willing to bear another's burden upon the weakening shoulders of his prayers.

While in England, Charles Alexander had insisted on taking Hyde to see his personal physician, who held a consultation with two other doctors. The doctors, realizing the seriousness of his condition, tried to impress this upon the preacher's mind. But Hyde, though willing to listen, was not eager to heed their advice to cease from his active prayer labors.

Alexander sat in on the advice-giving, and he with the doctors was amazed at Praying Hyde's composure. When told he was dying even then by degrees, his face dimmed with a serious glow, for he knew at last he was going home to be with the Lord, whom so many times he had glimpsed in vision.

And there was only one place where John wished to pass away, and that was in his homeland, which had given him birth. So he embarked for America, arriving in New York, August 8, 1911. At once he entrained for Clifton Springs, New York, where if possible he hoped to obtain relief from the serious headaches which had attacked him with trip-hammer severity for several years.

Upon examination physicians advised a brain-tumor operation. When the operation was performed the tumor was pronounced malignant, for which even the highest medical skill was not sufficient. Rallying for a while from the operation, he joined his sister on December 19 at Northampton, Massachusetts, where her husband Professor E. H. Mensel was engaged as teacher.

The malignant cancer again attacked him in his back and side. Thinking it was rheumatism, Hyde sought to have it relieved, but the doctors knew it was the cancer cropping out once more with greater ferocity than before.

When February dawned, the outer man of Praying Hyde had rapidly wasted away, and the physical anguish he then bore matched well the spiritual agony of his many intercessory years. Even to the end he carried this prayer burden. For on October 27, 1911, he had written, "I am still in bed or wheelchair, getting a fine rest and doing a lot of the ministry of intercession, and having not a few opportunities of personal work. How the radiance of holiness shone out in Jesus' every word and deed."

He had paid the price and now the last word of the record of his earthly pilgrimage was being written. On February 17, 1912, while suffering intense pain, his face lighted with a radiant glow as God opened his lips for a final pean of praise.

"Bol, Yisu Masih, Ki Jai!" he shouted as his earthly trek closed and his heavenly career began — "Shout the victory of Jesus Christ!" Closing his eyes to time's vain attractions, he opened them to behold Jesus in all His eternal glory.

Praying Hyde's days were at an end, but not his influence, for his dying shout — *"Bol, Yisu Masih, Ki Jai"* — has become the battle cry of the Punjab Church.

Dr. W. B. Anderson, writing later, affords us a vision of Praying Hyde's enlarged sphere of intercession. "He went a long way," he says, "into the suffering of India, and he had desperate encounters with her foes for deliverance . . . Speaking intimately to intimate friends Hyde said, 'On the day of prayer God gave me a new experience. I seemed to be away above our conflict here in the Punjab and I saw God's great battle in all India, and then away out beyond in China, Japan and Africa.

" 'I saw how we had been thinking in narrow circles . . . and how God was joining rapidly force to force and line to line and all was beginning to be one great struggle. That to me means the final triumph of Christ . . . We must exercise care to be utterly obedient to Him who sees all the battlefield . . . !' "

This world vision had at that time engulfed his intercessory life, and he who had labored almost twenty years in India was also to bear the burdens of the whole world.

His sister Mary accompanied the body to the old home in Carthage, Illinois, that the funeral might be spoken from the pulpit where John as a young man had heard his father's voice ring forth in pleading prayer and triumphant sermon for God to send workers into the ripened harvest — a prayer which John himself was to help answer.

The Rev. J. F. Young, a classmate, then pastor of the church, preached the dedicatory sermon by which the bones of Praying Hyde were laid to rest in the bosom of the earth awaiting the morn of resurrection. Assisting in the pulpit was Francis McGaw, who was to write the first American sketch of his friend John's life.

"It was my privilege . . . to look down into the casket on that dear, dear face," says McGaw. "He was greatly emaciated, but it was the same sweet, peaceful, gentle yet strong, resolute face that I had known in 1901, the last time I saw him alive."

Under that cloud-ridden sky on a gloomy day, February 20, John's body was escorted to the Moss Ridge Cemetery, where a freshly dug grave, by the side of those of his father, mother and brother Edmund, was ready to receive his mortal remains.

Eulogistic words were spoken on that day, yet they could add little to the luster of Praying Hyde's name, which already had been brightened by his constant entrance into the Holy of holies where he talked with his Lord.

His last request had been that $5,000 be raised to build a preacher's home at Moga, where his work had finally been centered. This task was bequeathed to Martha Gray, who through the years of his India ministry had assisted in raising money for his support. "Tell Miss Gray," he had said, "to ask the Carthage Church and the Christian Endeavor Societies of Rushville Presbytery for $5,000 to build a missionary bungalow in Moga for the workers.''

"Homeless himself," Miss Gray adds, "he craved a home for those who should come after him."

The Board of Foreign Missions, Presbyterian Church, said of him: "Mr. Hyde was one of the most devout, prayerful, and fruitful missionary workers in India. With no adoption of native dress or external signs of asceticism, he was recognized by the India people as a 'Holy Man,' who knew God and the deepest secrets of life, and they came to him in unreserved confidence and trust."

Martha Gray, true to this dying request, began raising the memorial fund, and year by year sums were added until when the final report was made in 1917, five years after Hyde had gone Home, she had raised $5,070, with which the Hyde Memorial Home was erected in Moga.

Out there in the Punjab, under the shadow of the Himalayas, the spirit of Praying Hyde hovers over the work to which his prayers gave birth. His influence waters the streams flowing therefrom to sweeten India's life and join with the River of Life, on whose eternal banks John now rests from his labors, and his works do follow him.